JESUS CHRIST: the Number of His Name

Other Books by Bonnie Gaunt

Time and the Bible's Number Code

The Stones and the Scarlet Thread

The Bible's Awesome Number Code

Beginnings: the Sacred Design

The Great Pyramid: Window on the Universe

The Magnificent Numbers of the Great Pyramid and Stonehenge

Stonehenge...a closer look

Available from:
Adventures Unlimited, Inc.
P.O. Box 74
Kempton, IL 60946
815-253-6390
auphq@frontiernet.net
www.adventuresunlimitedpress.com

JESUS CHRIST
the Number of His Name

The Amazing Number Code
Hidden in the Bible

Bonnie Gaunt

Adventures Unlimited Press
Kempton, IL 60946, U.S.A.

Adventures Unlimited Press
P.O. Box 74
Kempton, IL 60946, U.S.A.
auphq@frontiernet.net
www.adventuresunlimitedpress.com

Manufactured in the United States of America

ISBN 0-932813-60-7

Library of Congress Card No. 98-092864

Hebrew Gematria is based on the Masoretic Text
Greek Gematria is based on the Nestle Text

Foreword

It was thirty years ago, at a Bible conference on the campus of Colorado State University, that a friend told me about gematria. My first response was, "No way!" It did not seem possible that numbers–empty symbols of amount–could possibly convey a message.

I remember walking, that afternoon, enjoying the beauty of the distant snow covered mountains, and basking in the awareness of the greatness of God. Snow covered mountains do that to me. But I could not get the concept of gematria out of my mind. I was curious.

Upon returning home to Michigan, I decided to see for myself if gematria was a pseudo-science, or if there could be any evidence that it contained a God-given message, encoded there into His word. Fortunately I had the Hebrew text of the Old Testament and the Greek text of the New Testament in my library, so, with calculator in hand, I began my search.

The first tears rolled down my face when I realized that the number equivalent for the name Lord Jesus Christ was the same as the measure of a square drawn on earth's diameter. It was either a colossal coincidence, or it was put there by a Master Mathematician. The same number, the number of His name, kept showing up in many other places. I could not consign it to coincidence. It was obviously intentional. The numbers were no longer empty symbols of amount; they were telling a beautiful story. They were telling of the unfathomable mind of the Creator–the one who plans for an eternity.

Not owning a computer, I set out to search the scriptures with my little calculator in hand. First I needed to know if there were any number patterns or if it was seemingly random. Not even knowing what numbers to look for, I simply added the number equivalents of everything that looked like it might be significant, and compiled it in numerical order into notebooks. Before long, the patterns emerged. Certain numbers were appearing over and over again, in words and phrases that had the same meaning. The patterns were multiples of 6, multiples of 8, multiples of 12; and to my surprise, multiples of 37 all seemed to pertain to both the Father and the Son and the work of creation and restoration–the reconciling of man to God.

I'm still compiling and adding to those notebooks. And, even though I now own a computer, I do not have the necessary software with which to do a complete search, so I'm still doing it with my little calculator.

Through the years, I have written and published five books in which I have shared the beauty of the numbers and the story they tell. This one is my sixth. The numbers are in perfect harmony with the basic building blocks of creation–the periodic table of the elements. They tell the story of creation and of the Creator. It was all encoded into the original text of the Bible, by the magnificent mind of the Creator.

In 1997 I became acquainted with the best seller, *The Bible Code,* by Michael Drosnin. He describes yet another code that is found in the text of the Old Testament, which has been called the ELS Code (Equidistant Letter Sequence). His search of the Code enabled him to predict the assassination of Prime Minister Yitzhak Rabin more than a year before it became a dreadful reality.

I was curious to see if the ELS Code would also work with the concept of gematria. Just as a logical starting place, I chose the best known text of the Old Testament which tells of the coming of the Messiah, Isaiah 9:6. We read it every Christmas– *"Unto us a Child is born, unto us a Son is given..."* I took the whole verse and used a skip-7 sequence, simply because the number seven sounded like a logical number to try. I pulled out every seventh Hebrew letter in the text and assigned its number equivalent, then added them with my calculator. When I looked at the answer the tears again rolled down my face. It was 888. The name Jesus, as is used throughout the New Testament, adds to 888. Into the very prophecy that told of his birth, was encoded his name, by the combination of both the ELS Code and gematria! As I wiped the tears from my eyes, I wondered if it might not be simply a coincidence and not master-minded after all.

As I turned pages in my Hebrew text of Isaiah, my eyes fell on another prophecy of Jesus, in chapter 11:1. "I wonder what this one will show," I thought, as I began pulling out every seventh Hebrew letter and adding their totals.

When I saw the answer on my calculator I was stunned. It was 888. I began jumping up and down and shouting, "It's real! It's real!"

In Michael Drosnin's search using his computer program of the ELS Code, he found, encoded into the text, the Hebrew years 5760 and 5766 as being significant years relating to Armageddon. I had previously found that the number 5760 in the gematria of the text also pointed to the second coming of Jesus, and his fulfilling of the prophecies regarding the King who will sit on David's throne. It appears that the time of His return has been encoded into the text.

I had not planned to write a sixth book. My circumstances and health did not present it as a wise task to pursue. Yet, my heart is so overflowing with joy I cannot contain it–I simply must share it with others. Thus I attempt another book. It is my hope and prayer that you, the reader, will find in this work the realization of the greatness and the majesty of God, and a joy in seeing another evidence of His work.

Bonnie Gaunt
1998

Contents

1
Number: the Language of the Universe

In A.D. 1963, astronomers in Green Bank, West Virginia pointed a giant saucer-shaped antenna at two remote stars, *Tau Ceti* and *Epsilon Eridani*. They were indeed listening for a message from outer space.

These were not visionary amateurs. The project was a sincere attempt to receive a message–if one were there– from extraterrestrial beings.

If such un-earthly beings did actually exist, and if they did attempt to communicate with earthlings, what language would they use? After pondering the problem, the astronomers concluded the only language that would make sense to all intelligent forms of life, anywhere in the universe, would be a mathematical one.

Mathematics, they said, is not so much a body of knowledge as it is a special kind of language. One so perfect and abstract that it could be understood by any intelligent creatures, existing anywhere. The grammar of the language is simple logic, and the vocabulary of the language are simple symbols–basically numerals that represent numbers.

As children, we were taught numerals as if they were dead symbols of amount. Their function as a language was not part of our journey through the three Rs. Thus, their function as a language does not find in us a response of recognition. And for this we are the poorer.

Not so in ancient times. Pythagoras, the 5th century B.C. mathematician, said "Numbers are the language of the universe." And he taught his students their importance as a language. Indeed, numbers are the very building blocks of creation–but they are much more than this. They are a language that communicates through time and space–an external language–a language of beginning.

Plato perceived the language of numbers and some of its messages planted in the universe. And he was aware of its source. "God ever geometrizes," he wrote. The British physicist, Sir James Jeans, declared, "The Great Architect of the universe now begins to appear as a pure mathematician."

To you and me, he does not send a "beep-beep-beep" or a "dot-dot-dash" from somewhere out in space, but he has left his great catalog of sacred information for us, concealed in number, planted in the universe, and in his written word. The prophet Isaiah gave us a glimpse of this when he wrote:

> *"To whom then will ye liken God? or what*
> *likeness will ye compare to him...? Have*
> *ye not known? Have ye not heard? Hath it*
> *not been told you from the beginning? Have*
> *ye not understanding from the foundation*
> *of the earth? It is he that sitteth upon the*
> *circle of the earth...; that stretcheth out the*

*heavens as a curtain, and spreadeth them
out as a tent to dwell in.... Lift up your eyes
on high, and behold who hath created these
things, that bringeth out their host by number..."* (Isaiah 40:18-26)

From the atom to the galaxy in the heavens, the same
unchanging laws apply–the laws of arithmetic, the language of number. Just as the hand of God spread the vast
expanse of the heavens by number, so too, his written word
can be reduced to number; and those who have tried it
have stood in awe of the intricacy and beauty of its
design. It was an intentional design.

In the year 547 B.C. a man named Daniel, a Hebrew
captive in Babylon, was given a vision which carried him
into the vast unknown future. At the conclusion of the
vision he saw two un-earthly creatures who spoke concerning the time when the vision would be fulfilled. One
of these creatures was identified by the name *Palmoni*. It
is a Hebrew word which means The Wonderful Numberer,
or The Numberer of Secrets. Daniel, being a Hebrew,
would have been aware of the importance of the name.
He was also aware of the language of number that was a
vital part of his native tongue.

Hebrew is probably the oldest language known to man.
It was a "dual character system" –a meaning of sound and
a meaning of number. It is the language of the Old Testament. Thus that wonderful old book, owned by nearly

3

every Christian the world over, is not only an historical record of man's relationship with his Creator, it is also a storehouse of secrets, locked up in number. The Numberer of Secrets who spoke to Daniel knew and used the language of number, the language of the universe.

Today, this use of number in scripture is largely forgotten. However, to the writers of the books of the Old Testament, it was a vital part of their knowledge, as well as a marvelous part of the heritage that has come down to us from their hand.

One of the best known demonstrations of this number code are the section headings in the 119th Psalm. Any student of the Old Testament is aware that the names for these sections are in fact the sequential letters of the Hebrew alphabet. It was their way of numbering the sections. Arabic numerals, such as we use today, were not known. The letters of their alphabet were used as numerals. The process was really quite simple and easy to understand.

The Hebrew alphabet uses 22 letters, with the addition of extended characters for some of the finals. In other words, if a character appeared within a word it would be written differently than if it appeared at the end of a word. These finals were given alternative numbers. However, in my study of the use of Hebrew as a numbering system in the original text, I find no use of the alternate numbers for the finals. It appears that these alternate numbers were not used originally, but came into use at a later date. Here is a simple, easy to use table by which anyone can find the number equivalents for the Hebrew text of the Old Testament.

Name	Letter	Value
Aleph	א	1
Beth	ב	2
Gimmel	ג	3
Daleth	ד	4
He	ה	5
Vau	ו	6
Zayn	ז	7
Cheth	ח	8
Teth	ט	9
Yod	י	10
Kaph	ך כ	20
Lamed	ל	30
Mem	ם מ	40
Nun	ן נ	50
Camek	ס	60
Ayin	ע	70
Pe	ף פ	80
Tsady	צ ץ	90
Qoph	ק	100
Reysh	ר	200
Sin	ש	300
Tau	ת	400

JESUS CHRIST: THE NUMBER OF HIS NAME

By using this number code, it is apparent that any word, name or phrase in the Old Testament has a number equivalent. It might be thought, on first glance, that this would be wholly random; however, it has been known by those who study this method of interpretation, that amazing number relationships can be observed that are far beyond the realm of random or even coincidence. Obvious and beautiful number patterns occur which are so remarkable that even the would-be skeptic is astonished. In it can be found the marvelous and magnificent mind of the Creator!

And it is not just the Old Testament that contains this amazing number code. The very same principle can be used with the Greek text of the New Testament. Moreover, the same number patterns exist interchangeably, between the Hebrew text and the Greek text, attesting to the existence of a single author–the mind of the Creator.

Among those who have searched into this vast and fathomless mine of gems, was the noted Bible expositor, E. W. Bullinger, whose work *Number in Scripture*, first published in 1894, shows the supernatural design in the use of numbers, both in the works of God and in the word of God. Closely following his work was the brilliant expose' of this number code by William Stirling in his book, *The Canon,* first published in 1897. He showed the undeniable connection between the numbers of the Bible and the geometry of the universe. In more recent years, the work of Jerry Lucas and Del Washburn, *Theomatics* (God's numbers), have brought to our attention the simplicity of the number patterns and their obvious divine origin.

This method of scripture interpretation is called by the Greek term *"gematria."* I first became aware of the use of gematria in the Bible in 1968. In the years since then, it has been an all-absorbing love that has led me into the search for the hidden message that the mind of the Creator has encoded into his witten word. The amazing gems that have been found have prompted me to write several books on the subject, this being the sixth.[1]

In this work, my focus will be on Jesus Christ, and the numbers that are used in his name. If there is any doubt or hint of unbelief that the numbers were encoded into the original text by the mind of the Creator, I hope to be able to spread the evidence upon the table, and let it eloquently speak for itself.

Let's look, for a moment, at the Greek alphabet. It is very similar in many ways to the Hebrew alphabet, and obviously is an extension of it. However, the Greek alphabet uses vowels, whereas the Hebrew does not. In Hebrew, the vowels are indicated by "pointings." The Greek alphabet contains 24 letters. Originally, it contained 26, however, two have fallen out of use through time. The alphabet, as used in the text of the New Testament, does

---

1   Other books by Bonnie Gaunt using the gematria of the Bible: *Beginnings: the Sacred Design,* 1995; *Stonehenge and the Great Pyramid: Window on the Universe,* 1993; *The Stones Cry Out,* 1991; *The Magnificent Numbers of the Great Pyramid and Stonehenge,* 1985; and *Stonehenge...a closer look,* 1979.

not contain the two obsolete letters, with one exception which will be shown later. Even its number code is nearly identical to the Hebrew.

Alpha	α	1
Beta	β	2
Gamma	γ	3
Delta	δ	4
Epsilon	ε	5
Zeta	ζ	7
Eta	η	8
Theta	θ	9
Iota	ι	10
Kappa	κ	20
Lambda	λ	30
Mu	μ	40
Nu	ν	50
Xi	ξ	60
Omicron	o	70
Pi	π	80
Rho	ρ	100
Sigma	$\sigma\ \varsigma$	200
Tau	τ	300
Upsilon	υ	400
Phi	ϕ	500
Chi	χ	600
Psi	ψ	700
Omega	ω	800

The two letters that have fallen out of use had the number values of 6 and 90. The letter-number 90 is not used in the New Testament, and the letter-number 6 is only used once, for a very special reason. The number 6 is the value of the letter *Stigma,* which looks nearly identical to the letter *Sigma.* It is used in Revelation 13:18 when giving the number of the beast. In the original manuscript, the number of the beast was written in gematria, using the three letters $\chi\xi\varsigma'$, which stand for 600, 60, and 6 respectively (adding to 666).

As an example of how this numbering system works, let's look at the best known name in the New Testament—the Lord Jesus Christ. The gematria for his name is demonstrated thus:

K	=	20		I	=	10		X	=	600
υ	=	400		η	=	8		ρ	=	100
ρ	=	100		σ	=	200		ι	=	10
ι	=	10		o	=	70		σ	=	200
o	=	70		υ	=	400		τ	=	300
ς	=	200		ς	=	200		o	=	70
		800				888		ς	=	200
										1480

Lord	=	800
Jesus	=	888
Christ	=	1480
		3168

JESUS CHRIST: THE NUMBER OF HIS NAME

The language of the universe is indeed the language of number. Its universal understanding will be found to be the language of the Bible.

That old Bible, that has come down to us from ancient times, carries within its pages a secret code that unlocks its treasures and its wonders, and through its pages we find a theme – that theme is the Lord Jesus Christ.

2
Jesus Christ and the Numbers of Creation

Three thousand years ago, King David expressed his wonder and reverence for the Creator when he penned the words:

> *"When I consider your heavens, the work of your fingers, the moon and the stars, which you have set in place, what is man that you are mindful of him?"*

Then David was so overwhelmed with the awesome beauty of the heavens that he simply burst forth:

> *"Oh Lord, our Lord, how majestic is your name in all the earth!"*

Looking up into the night sky is awesome indeed. It fills us with an awareness of the vastness of creation, and our own littleness in comparison.

The Apostle John, when speaking of the vastness of all creation said:

> *"In the beginning was the Word, and the Word was with God...He was with God in*

> *the beginning. Through him all things were*
> *made; without him nothing was made that*
> *has been made..."*

He was the maker of all things, and, just like a great artist, he has signed his name to all his works – that name is his number, 3168.

He made earth to be man's home, and by its very size it bears the number of his name.

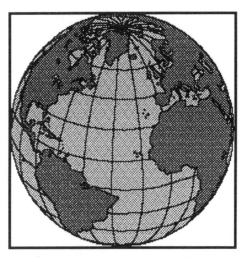

Perimeter of square 31,680 miles.

If someone were to draw a square all the way around the circle of the earth, enclosing the earth within, the measure of the square would be 31,680 miles.

Does it seem possible that he created the earth to bear the number of his name? It may sound like just a rare and meaningless coincidence, until we look further.

12

Only a small portion of the earth is habitable for man. Our home consists of the earth's crust, known as the lithosphere, and the air we breathe, known as the atmosphere. This thin layer of habitable conditions that surrounds our globe is comparable to the skin of an apple in relation to the size of the apple.

The average depth of the lithosphere is about ten miles. Below that is the molten magma which we see occasionally when it erupts from the bowels of a volcano.

The atmosphere is divided into layers. The troposphere extends upward from sea level approximately seven miles. Beyond that is the stratosphere, going up to twenty two miles. Temperatures in the troposphere decrease with altitude. In the stratosphere they are nearly constant. Above the stratosphere is the mesosphere, with temperatures decreasing with altitude. But after fifty miles above sea level, the temperature decrease abruptly stops. It acts as if there were a thin skin surrounding earth, fifty miles up. This imaginary skin is called the mesopause–it is the farthest reaches of earth's atmosphere. Thus the earth acts as if it were enclosed in a thermal balloon, fifty miles up.

Combine the 50 miles up with the 10 miles down, and the extent of man's home is 60 miles (vertical). Convert 60 miles to feet and it bears the number of its Maker, 3168 (60 x 5,280 = 316,800 feet).

Earth's biosphere is the only genuinely *living* system that we know of in the Universe. No single organism from that biosphere could continue to live outside of it. It is thrilling to realize that its very dimensions tell us of its Maker–the One upon whom life really depends.

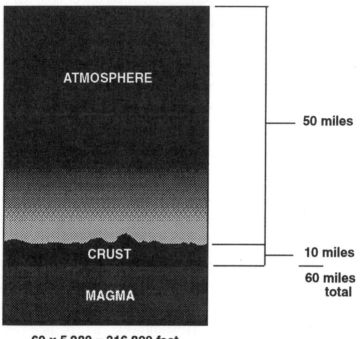

60 x 5,280 = 316,800 feet
3168 = Lord Jesus Christ

I cannot help but be reminded of the words of the Apostle Paul when he stood on Mars Hill above Athens. He said, *"In Him we live and move and have our being."* How true are his words. The air that we breathe and the ground that we walk upon bears his signature–the number of his name, 3168.

Every twenty four hours, as our earth makes one complete revolution, its surface is bathed in life-giving light from the sun. The prophet Malachi spoke of the time coming when *"The Sun of Righteousness will arise, with healing on his wings."* In the original Hebrew text, the prophet was not really making a play on words, but when translated into English, it provides a delightful homonym. It is the same concept that Jesus spoke of when he said *"I am the light of the world. Whoever follows me will never walk in darkness, but will have the light of life."* (John 8:12)

The light from the sun is indeed life-giving, and aptly represents the life which Jesus gave to us by taking the sinners place upon the cross. He is our light and our life.

How fitting, then, to realize that the actual distance that light comes to us from the sun bears the signature of its Maker, the one who died on that cross that we might have life.

If our earth were any further from the sun, or any nearer to the sun, human life could not exist on this planet. The Designer of the Universe has placed earth's distance from the sun at precisely the right place to support life. That distance is a mean of 93 million miles. I say "mean" because earth's orbit around the sun is eliptical, causing it to be nearer to the sun at certain times during the year than at others. However, the mean distance is 93 million miles.

If we were to convert those 93 million miles to inches,

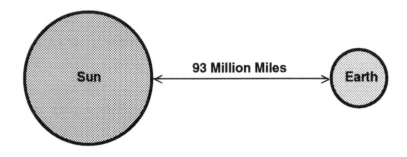

(Zeros dropped)
93 x 528 = 49,104 feet
49,104 x 12 = 589,248 inches
Speed of Light = 186,000 mps
589,248 ÷ 186 = <u>3,168</u>
Lord Jesus Christ = <u>3168</u>

Circumference of Earth 24,881.392 miles
589,248 ÷ 24,881.392 = <u>23.68</u>
Jesus Christ = <u>2368</u>

and divide by the speed of light, the figure that would result would be 3168, which is the gematria for the name Lord Jesus Christ. Moreover, if we divide that distance, stated in inches, by the circumference of the earth, the answer would be 2368, which is the gematria for Jesus Christ. It is too startling to be blind coincidence! It bears evidence that he of whom John said *"All things were made by him, and without him was nothing made,"* placed his signature there–the Number of His Name!

But look, for a moment, at the necessities for this reality. Not only must the earth be the right *distance* from the sun, both to provide life for man and to provide the Number of His Name, but the *size* of the earth must be exactly right, both to provide life for man and the Number of His Name. It is known that if the earth were smaller or larger, or closer or further from the sun, no life as we know it could exist. Truly *"In Him* (in His number) *we live and move and have our being."*

```
Lord Jesus Christ = 3168
Jesus Christ      = 2368
```

This amazing relationship of the sun to the earth is part of a larger closed system, which we call our Solar System. With the sun at its functional center, nine planets orbit around it, each in its own path, plane and distance.

The fact that there are only nine planets is significant because the number nine, as it relates to God's numbers, indicates a completion. The numbers 1 through 8 complete the octave and begin again; but the number 9 is additional and indicates completion. The last word in the Bible, and the word with which we complete a prayer, is *"Amen,"* and its gematria is 99.

One of the amazing features of the number 9 is its relationship to all the rest of the digits. If we multiplied 9 ones by 9 ones, the result would be a palindrome of all nine digits.

111111111 x 111111111 = 12345678987654321

The number nine completes the planetary activity surrounding our sun. The number nine indicates a wholeness. It also implies the ultimate manifestation of a concept or thing. This is the way the number nine is used in the scriptures. Its meaning is derived from its use.

About a hundred years ago, astronomers suspected that there was a tenth planet out there beyond Pluto. They had never seen it, but the irregular orbit of Neptune suggested there was something there. So they named it Planet X. In the 1950s some astronomers suggested that instead of an unknown planet beyond Pluto, perhaps there existed a belt of huge ice chunks surrounding the Solar System. They named it the Kuiper belt.

In August of 1992, a tiny reddish spot of light recorded on a sensitive electronic detector in Hawaii became the first component of the Kuiper belt ever observed. The existence of the Kuiper belt was suddenly changed from theory to fact. The new spot of light was named 1992 QB1.

Time magazine (September 28, 1992, p. 59) made the following observation about this discovery:

> Proof that the Kuiper belt exists would help demonstrate that another long-sought object almost certainly does not. For nearly a century, astronomers have been looking for Planet X, a

world conjectured to lie far beyond Pluto....
Planet X was first dreamed up to explain the
apparent irregularities in Neptune's orbit.
Recent studies have shown those irregularities
to be an illusion–and the sighting of QB1 has
probably dashed forever the hope of finding a
10th planet.[1]

Yes, 9 completes the planets, just as 9 completes the digits. The Encyclopedia Britannica lists the mean distance that light travels from the sun to each of these planets (dropping the zeros):

Mercury	36
Venus	67
Earth	93
Mars	142
Jupiter	483
Saturn	886
Uranus	1,782
Neptune	2,793
Pluto	3,672
	9,954

Thus the combined distances that light travels from the sun to each of the nine planets is 9,954 (dropping the zeros). Think of this number as representing the giant ball of our Solar System. If we were to draw a line directly through its middle, that line would measure 3,168.

1   Quoted by permission of Time, Inc., New York, NY.

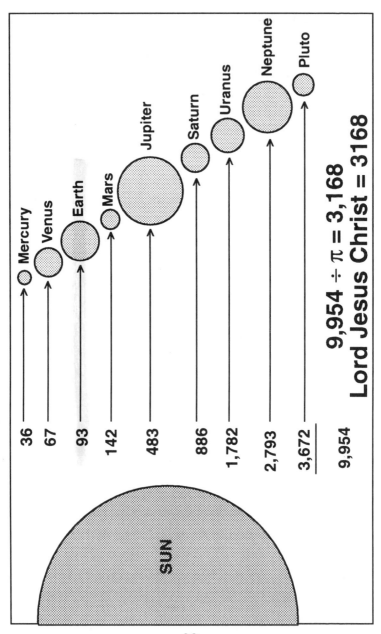

The amazing reality is that the whole Solar System, of which man's home is a small part, bears the number of its Maker. The Artist has signed his name to his work.

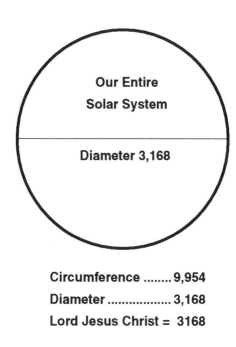

Circumference 9,954
Diameter 3,168
Lord Jesus Christ = 3168

That Artist left his glorious realm, and came to earth, in fulfillment of the prophecies, to die in Adam's stead, and thus redeem the Adamic race. And, just as the prophecies had predicted, he was born in the little town of Bethlehem. In the prophecies it was called *"Bethlehem Ephratah,"* which means *"The Fruitful House of Bread."* And indeed it was a fruitful house of bread, for in that small middle east village, the "Bread of Life" came to give himself for us, that we might have life. The prophet Micah told us of his coming.

> *"You, Bethlehem Ephratah, you who are little among the thousands of Judah, out of you He shall come forth to Me to be ruler in Israel, and His goings forth have been from of old, from the days of eternity."*

Little did Micah realize the importance of that prophecy to all mankind, or the significance of the spot on this entire globe where that Ruler would be born. Bethlehem sits at 31.68° N. latitude. It was no coincidence! He was born on the Number of His Name.

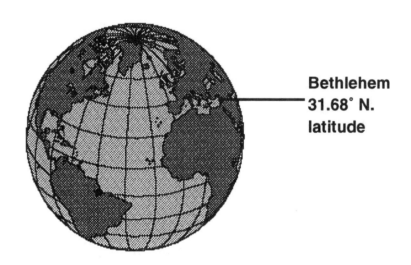

Bethlehem 31.68° N. latitude

Lord Jesus Christ = 3168

It has been shown (page 12) that a square drawn around the circle of the earth will have a perimeter of 31,680 miles. As the earth orbits the sun, it takes with it its very own satellite, the moon. Thus the earth and moon, in relation to the sun, become a unit, traveling together the 595 million miles of its orbit during a period of a little more than 365 days. For purposes of their geometry, let's consider the earth and moon as positioned tangent to each other, and enclose this unit in a circle. It is not coincidence that the circle which would enclose these two orbs has a circumference of 31,680 miles. Yes, again it bears the signature of its Maker, the Number of His Name.

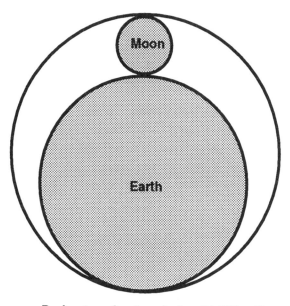

Perimeter of outer circle   31,680 miles
Lord Jesus Christ   =   3168

The earth is not only bathed in the light from the sun (solar light), but it is also gently caressed by the light from the moon. However, moonlight is actually reflected light from the sun. Both orbs play an important role in the gematria of the scriptures.

The sun, as it is spelled in the New Testement, $\eta\lambda\iota o\varsigma$, adds to 318, while the moon, $\sigma\epsilon\lambda\eta\nu\eta$, adds to 301. Thus the total gematria for both sun and moon is 619.

If we drew a circle whose circumference is 619, it will have a diameter of 197 – again calling attention to the child that was born in Bethlehem, for it was prophesied that he would be called Immanuel, עמנו אל = 197.

Sun = 318
Moon = 301
—————
619

Circumference 619

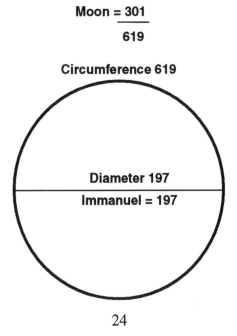

Diameter 197
Immanuel = 197

Although it was prophesied that his name would be called Immanuel, which means "God with us," his mother called him Jesus, as she was instructed. The name Jesus is the Greek form of the Hebrew name Joshua, meaning saviour. The name Jesus, as it is spelled in Greek, bears a very important number in the gematria of the scriptures. It is the triplet of 8s.

$$\text{Jesus } I\eta\sigma\sigma\upsilon\varsigma = 888$$

The orbit of the earth-moon unit around the sun covers an eliptical path of 595 million miles. If we were to roll that out into a straight line, and measure the time it would take light from the sun to traverse its full length, the result is amazing! Again, for this calculation we will drop all the zeros and decimal points as they only complicate the beauty of the numbers.

595 million miles ÷ 186 = 31989247 seconds
31989247 ÷ 60 = 533154 minutes
533154 ÷ 60 = 888 hours
Jesus, Iησους = 888

Truly the Artist has signed his name to all his works! Such evidence of design reveals the unfathomable mind of the Designer.

We are humbled with awe and reverence as we look up into the sky on a clear night and behold the works of his hands.

We can enter into the feelings of David as he looked up into the vastness and beauty of the night sky, and set his thoughts to music:

> *"The heavens declare the glory of God; the skies proclaim the work of his hands. Day after day they pour forth speech; night after night they display knowledge. There is no speech or language where their voice is not heard. Their voice goes out into all the earth, their words to the ends of the world."* (Psalm 19:1)

David was probably not aware that the words he chose bore the signature of the Artist who spread that vast array of stars before him.

The heavens declare the glory of God = 888

3
Jesus Christ - 3168

After the Israelites left their servitude in Egypt, they endured a desert journey that lasted forty years. Their leader, Moses, brought them to the border of the promised land, the land of Canaan, and there he died. His successor, Joshua, took them across the Jordan River and into the land that God had promised to them.

This large band of nomadic people now began to dispossess the natives of the land, and to settle in, plant fields, build homes, and set up their own governing process. Joshua (the Greek form of his name is Jesus), received instructions from God for the building of six very special cities that were to be strategically placed in various parts of the land. They were called Cities of Refuge.

The purpose of these cities was a benevolent one. It was a provision made for the person who had committed involuntary manslaughter, where he could find safety and refuge from the avenger. A person who had committed such a crime was allowed to flee to one of these Cities of Refuge, and as long as he lived within its boundaries, the avenger could not touch him.

Just as we often find, in God's dealings with man, the natural, physical realities often are illustrations of a spiritual, or higher concept. And so it is with the Cities of

Refuge. They were safe havens for the offender, as long as he remained within their boundaries.

The higher picture, or meaning, is obvious. Just as Adam sinned and brought the whole human family into a death penalty, so if an individual flees to a City of Refuge, representing Jesus Christ, he is safe from that penalty of death, and is offered the hope of life.

This is somewhat of an oversimplification of a much more involved story, but it will suffice to convey the principal concept of the Cities of Refuge. In a nutshell, they represent Jesus Christ.

These cities were to be laid out according to specific instructions regarding their size. They were to be a square within a square. The inner square was the city, and the outer square surrounding it was the suburb, used for pasturing their cattle and for gardens, etc. Each side of the suburbs measured 4,000 cubits, giving a perimeter of 16,000 cubits, while the city had sides of 2,000 cubits, making a perimeter of 8,000 cubits.

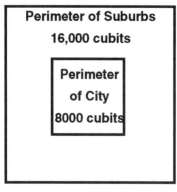

The cubit in use at that ancient date was the old Sumerian cubit of 19.8 inches. Using this cubit, it is observed that the perimeter of the suburbs of each of the Cities of Refuge measured 316,800 inches. Just as our refuge from Adamic death and our hope of life is in the Lord Jesus Christ, whose number is 3168, so in the illustration, the boundary of their protection bore the number 316,800.

As becomes apparent as we progress in this study, the dimensions of the Cities of Refuge were not random, and their identification with the Lord Jesus Christ was not a coincidence. It was part of a great master plan.

Coming down through time approximately 400 years, we find another piece of that plan identified in the construction of Solomon's Temple in Jerusalem. God gave Solomon instructions as to its dimensions, and even told him which cubit to use in its measure. He said to use the *"cubit of the old measure,"* – meaning the old Sumerian cubit that they had used back at the time of the building of the Cities of Refuge.

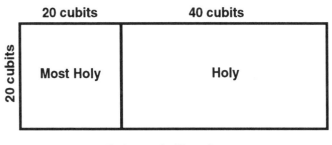

Solomon's Temple

Confirmation of the use of the 19.8 inch cubit in the building of the Temple can be found in the Encyclopedia Judaica. There it states that this was the "Temple cubit."

The perimeter of the ground plan of the Temple was 160 cubits. When we multiply this by the 19.8 inch cubit, the result is 3,168 inches.

The Temple was the meeting place between man and God, just as the Lord Jesus Christ, whose number is 3168, is the meeting place, or means by which man can be restored to the life and *"sonship"* that was lost in Adam. The Temple was the place of reconciliation. The Lord Jesus Christ is the means of our reconciliation to God. The use of the Number of His Name was no coincidence–it was part of a beautiful master plan.

The accomplishment of that reconciliation is pictured by two more cities–Ezekiel's City, and the New Jerusalem.

Ezekiel's City is not as well known to students of the Bible as is the New Jerusalem, therefore it might be helpful to get a little of the background regarding this magnificent city.

Ezekiel lived in Jerusalem in the days when Jehoiakim was king of the little nation of Judah. When Jehoiakim died, his young son Jehoiachin became king. It was in that year that king Nebuchadnezzar, of Babylon, laid siege to Jerusalem and took Jehoiachin captive to Babylon–and he took Ezekiel with him.

Ezekiel was a priest, and his ministry in the Temple

was the whole thrust of his life. Being deported to a land 700 miles away, and a heathen land at that, was an indescribable trauma in his life. But it was made even worse by the fact that his captors separated him from his small children. Ezekiel and his wife were forced to leave their young children behind in Jerusalem when they were transported to the far away city of Babylon.

After four long years in his land of separation, Ezekiel was given a vision, in which he was told of the impending doom of Jerusalem, and of his beloved Temple. His deep grief was overwhelming. He thought of his children that had been kept in Jerusalem, and grieved for their safety. And he grieved for his beloved Temple, the meeting place between God and man. That it would be destroyed was unthinkable! Yet, this is what the vision told him.

In the vision he heard a voice telling him, *"Write thee the name of the day, even this same day; the King of Babylon set himself against Jerusalem this same day."*

But, as it turned out, the tragedy of that day was a very personal one for Ezekiel, for on that same day, his wife died. He was left alone in a foreign land, and he longed for the safety of his children who were left in Jerusalem.

For fourteen long years in the city of his captivity, Ezekiel mourned the loss of the beautiful Temple. He wondered, would there ever again be a meeting place between God and man?

Then one day, he had another vision, but unlike the bad news of the first vision, this vision bore glorious news. It showed him a new Temple, and there was a beautiful river that flowed out from the Temple. Then he was taken in the vision to a high mountain where he looked down on a beautiful and glorious city which was spread out on the valley below. The city was laid out as a huge square, with three gates on each side, and on each gate was the name of one of the 12 tribes of Israel.

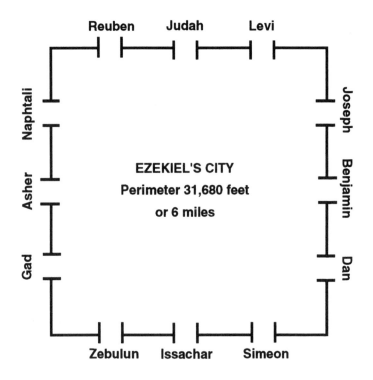

To Ezekiel the vision was a confirmation of all that he had lived for—it was the assurance that there would be once again a meeting place between God and man. To students of the Old Testament, the vision is a promise of redemption from the Adamic death-curse, and a reconciliation to God. It is a beautiful picture of the relationship of man to his Creator during and beyond earth's great millennium.

Ezekiel was told to measure the Temple and the City. But he was given a very special instrument for measurement. He was told to use a *"reed"* that was six great cubits in length. This great cubit was to be different than the cubit then in use. Ezekiel was in Babylon, and he was instructed to use the Babylonian *"moderate cubit"* plus a handbreadth. The combined length of this special cubit was comparable in our measures to 1.76 feet. Six of these would be the reed of 10.56 feet in length.

The measure around the perimeter of the City was 18,000 great cubits. Thus, 18,000 x 1.76 = 31,680 feet, or 5,280 reeds – the same number of reeds as there are feet in our British mile. The City bore the signature of the Lord Jesus Christ, whose number is 3168. It was a picture of the reconciliation of man to God through the Lord Jesus Christ.

The same picture is given to us in the Book of Revelation, but the city is called the New Jerusalem. The Apostle John saw this city in vision also, and he described it in beautiful pictorial language:

> *"I saw the Holy City, the New Jerusalem,*
> *coming down out of heaven from God,*
> *prepared as a bride, beautifully dressed for*

33

her husband. And I heard a loud voice from the throne saying, 'Now the dwelling of God is with men, and he will live with them. They will be his people, and God himself will be with them and be their God. He will wipe every tear from their eyes. There will be no more death or mourning or crying or pain, for the old order of things has passed away.' ...And he carried me away in the Spirit to a mountain great and high, and showed me the Holy City, Jerusalem, coming down out of heaven from God. It shone with the glory of God, and its brilliance was like that of a very precious jewel, like a jasper, clear as crystal. It had a great, high wall with twelve gates, and with twelve angels at the gates. On the gates were written the names of the twelve tribes of Israel. There were three gates on the east, three on the north, three on the south and three on the west. The wall of the city had twelve foundations, and on them were the names of the twelve apostles of the Lamb."

The similarity of the description to that of Ezekiel's city is apparent. It was square, and had three gates on each side, with the names of each of the tribes of Israel on the gates. However, the New Jerusalem had an added feature

– its height was equal to its width and length. This describes a cube.

Each side of this cube was 12,000 furlongs. There are 660 feet in a furlong, thus 660 x 12,000 = 7,920,000 per side, multiplied by four gives the perimeter of the New Jerusalem as 31,680,000 feet. It bore the signature of the Lord Jesus Christ. And it is only through means of his redeeming blood that man will ever come into the conditions pictured by this glorious city.

But there is something startling about the description of this City. It is said that its wall measured 144 cubits. This tells us that the wall must have been circular, for it would take 144 royal cubits to measure a circle that would fit within the square whose sides are 12,000 furlongs each. (If it were indeed the royal cubit of 1.72 feet.)

However, if the City is a cube, then the circular wall may be a sphere. If it is, then that sphere would be commensurate with the sphere of our earth, for its diameter is the same but to a different scale.

The implications are thrilling! John might possibly have been describing a condition that will come down and engulf the whole earth. Pictorially it is given as the same measurements as our earth, but merely to a different scale. And symbolically it could be saying that this New Jerusalem is, in actuality, a condition that will engulf our whole planet – showing man's full reconciliation to God.

Some have interpreted the description of the New Jerusalem as that of a pyramid, which could have its four sides and its height of equal measure. The scripture does not really settle that question. However, since its measures are identical with the measures of our earth, it seems reasonable to suggest that the New Jerusalem is a cube, representing our entire earth and the peoples on it.

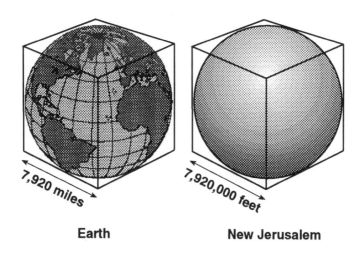

Earth

New Jerusalem

Perimeter of Earth square 31,680 miles
Perimeter of New Jerusalem 31,680,000 feet
Lord Jesus Christ = 3168

4
Jesus Christ: The Branch

Jesus Christ has many titles. One of the prophetic titles that has been used of him is The Branch. There is a consistency among several of the writers of Old Testament books concerning the use of this name. Isaiah spoke of The Branch sometime between approximately 760 to 700 B.C. More than a hundred years passed before the prophet Jeremiah wrote about The Branch. After Jeremiah, another seventy years went by before the prophet Zechariah again spoke of The Branch.

It is evident that these writers were not collaborating and deciding upon a name to use for this prophetic character, for they did not live contemporaneously.

But why would a Messianic prophecy assign to him such a strange name?

God had given the promise to David that his dynasty would be an everlasting one. The root of this dynasty was David (and sometimes it is mentioned as Jesse, David's father), and the tree that grew up were his successors on the throne of Judah. But the tree was cut down in 586 B.C. when the army of Nebuchadnezzar burned the city of Jerusalem and took many of the people captive to Babylon. But it was prophesied that a *"Branch"* would grow up out of the *"stump"* of David. It is called a stump because the tree had been cut down. The stump remained because God had promised that the dynasty would be forever; therefore the stump was the promise. As long as there was a stump left, there was hope that the tree could grow again. And God always keeps his promises!

The prophet Isaiah described this glorious Branch:

> *"A shoot will come up from the stump of Jesse; from his roots a Branch will bear fruit. The Spirit of the Lord will rest on him— the spirit of wisdom and of understanding, the Spirit of counsel and of power, the Spirit of knowledge and of the fear of the Lord.... He will not judge by what he sees with his eyes, or decide by what he hears with his ears; but with righteousness he will judge the needy, with justice he will give decisions for the poor of the earth.... Righteousness will be his belt and faithfulness the sash around his waist.... In that day the Root of Jesse will stand as a banner for the peoples; the nations will rally to him, and his place of rest will be glorious. "* (Isaiah 11)

Isaiah was looking down through time, not to the baby that was born in Bethlehem, but to the glorious time when the Messiah would be king over all the earth. Other prophecies tell us that when Messiah comes as a king, he will sit on the throne of David; in other words, he will be the promised king who will be of the Davidic line–the dynasty of David.

He did come first as the baby in Bethlehem because it was necessary that he first offer himself as man's redeemer. He must first pay the death penalty for Adam, thereby releasing man from its curse, and purchasing for them the promise of life that Adam had lost. But when he comes again, he comes as a King. This is why the Apostle Paul said, *"There is one God, and one Mediator between God and men, the man Christ Jesus, who gave himself a ransom for all."* To confirm the identity of this *"Mediator between God and men,"* we again go to the gematria. In the Greek text the letter-numbers of this title add to 3168 – exactly the same number as the name Lord Jesus Christ.

When he was here, he called himself by yet another name. He often referred to himself as the Son of Man. This was because he was calling attention to the fact that he was a child of Adam through his mother, Mary, while still evidencing that he was the Son of God. The two were necessary for the work that he was to accomplish–the work of purchasing man from the Adamic death penalty. It is fitting, therefore, that the name by which he called himself–The Son of Man, η υιου του ανθρωπου–adds to 3168. It is the Number of His Name.

The name by which we know him best–Lord Jesus Christ– is spelled several ways in the Greek text. This is because in the Greek language words and names are often spelled differently according to their placement in a sentence. The name Jesus Christ is spelled two ways, and as if to place emphasis on the importance of the number, both of these spellings add to the same number, 2368.

2368 = Jesus Christ, *Ιησους Χριστος*
2368 = Jesus Christ, *Ιησου Χριστου*

The different spellings for Lord Jesus Christ do *not* add to the same number.

 800 = Lord, *Κυριος*
1000 = Lord, *Κυριου*

3168 = Lord Jesus Christ, *Κυριος Ιησους Χριστος*
3368 = Lord Jesus Christ, *Κυριου Ιησους Χριστος*

Observing how the numbers match is always a thrill to me. And it was especially so when I added the letter-numbers for The Branch. To find the gematria of The Branch and the Lord Jesus Christ identical was a strong confirmation, not only that it is identifying the same person, but that the whole concept of gematria is a valid concept, and one obviously used by God in his written word.

The first mention of The Branch was in Isaiah 4:2. It reads, *"In that day will the Branch of Jehovah be beautiful and glorious, and the fruit of the earth for pride and for glory for the survivors of Israel."* It adds to 3368, just as does the second spelling of Lord Jesus Christ. But there are other interesting things in the gematria of this verse that continue to identify it.

If we pull out certain phrases, as the words appear consecutively in the original text, we get the following:

296 = The Branch of Jehovah, beautiful
296 = and the fruit
<u>296</u> = of the earth
888

Each of these adds to 296, and when added together they total 888. The name Jesus in Greek adds to 888. The use of the number 296 three times consecutively in this verse caught my attention because of the other uses of this number in the gematria of the scriptures. It obviously is a number that refers to Jesus. Here are a few of them.

296 = Only begotten, $\mu o v o \gamma \varepsilon v \eta$
296 = He shall appear in His glory, נראה בכבודו
2960 = Son of Man, $\upsilon \iota o \varsigma \tau o \upsilon \alpha v \theta \rho \omega \pi o \upsilon$

Another item that came to my attention when studying the gematria of Isaiah 4:2 is that if we removed the description *"beautiful and glorious"* the rest of the text would add to 3168. The extra 200 for *"beautiful and glorious"* matches the extra 200 for the alternate spelling of Lord in the Greek text. Thus, this statement of Isaiah concerning The Branch, bears the numbers for both spellings of Lord Jesus Christ, 3168 and 3368.

Approximately 200 years after Isaiah wrote this prophecy, Zechariah recorded the words of the Lord that were given to him.

> *"The Man whose name is The Branch, He*
> *shall grow up out of His place, and He shall*
> *build the Temple of Jehovah."* (Zech. 6:12)

The letter-numbers of the Hebrew text add to 2368. The name Jesus Christ, by both its Greek spellings, adds to 2368. By the gematria of the Hebrew text, Zechariah's prophecy identifies the man called The Branch.

Wherever this title is used in the prophetic scriptures, it has reference to the Lord Jesus Christ, in his role as the successor of David–the promised King who would sit on David's throne. It was promised that his kingdom would last forever.

5
Jesus Christ and the Golden Proportion

It has long been an item of wonder and speculation: why did Joseph and Mary travel to Bethlehem at the time when she was due to deliver her child? Surely she knew the time of her delivery. To make such a trip at that late date in her pregnancy was not to be an ordinary event, or one to be thought lightly of. She was very young–a teenager– and this was her first pregnancy. To risk the hardships of traveling by donkey or on foot, to a place that was strange to her, not knowing where she would deliver or under what circumstances, was unusual to say the least; and for some, who have had difficult deliveries, this trip might seem like a very unwise move.

The prophecies, however, foretold that the son of the virgin would be born in Bethlehem. We don't know if Mary was aware of this. We do know that she was aware of the very specialness of this child, for she had been told by the angel, Gabriel, *"You will be with child and give birth to a son, and you are to give him the name Jesus. He will be great and will be called the Son of the Most High. The Lord God will give him the throne of his father David, and he will reign over the house of Jacob forever; his kingdom will never end."* (Luke 1:31-33)

43

JESUS CHRIST: THE NUMBER OF HIS NAME

On page 22 it has been shown that the latitude of Bethlehem is 31.68° North. That latitude bore the Number of His Name. It is worthy of note that the latitude of 31.68° N is located on our globe at just the right distance from the Equator to produce a Golden Rectangle. The relationship of the location of Bethlehem to earth's equatorial diameter and its polar diameter forms a Golden Rectangle. It is not likely a coincidence, especially when we take into consideration the other occurrences of the Number of His Name in all creation.

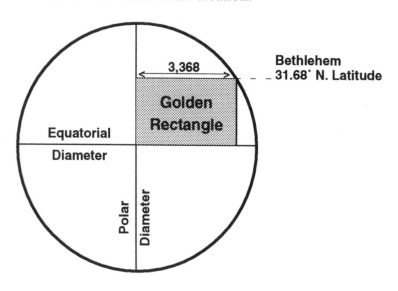

Mean radius of earth (diagonal of rectangle) = 3,960 miles

Long side of Golden Rectangle   = 3,368 miles

Lord Jesus Christ, *Κυριου Ιησους Χριστος* = 3368

Latitude of Bethlehem   = 31.68° N

Lord Jesus Christ, *Κυριος Ιησους Χριστος* = 3168

Take a good look at that diagram. It is nothing short of fantastic! It is based upon the mean diameter of the earth in relation to its radius of 3,960 miles, and also in relation to the latitude of Bethlehem. These relationships produce the Golden Rectangle, and the Number of His Name by both its spellings. It is nothing that I have contrived. It is the Number of His Name that was planted in the geometry of our earth from the beginning. No wonder it was necessary that Mary give birth to her baby in Bethlehem! That precise spot on earth bears the Number of His Name and gives witness that both spellings, as are used throughout the New Testament, are divinely ordained.

But that's not all! There is longitude to be considered also. The longitude of Bethlehem is 35.2° E. If we were to multiply this by the number of completion, 9, the product would be 3168 (not considering decimal points).

Shortly before his death, Jesus told his disciples that he would go away, but he would return and take them to be with him. Then he made a rather strange statement: he said, *"You know the way to the place where I am going."* However, the disciples did not know the way, or so they thought, so they asked him, *"Lord, we don't know where you are going, so how can we know the way?"*

To this Jesus replied, *"I am the way, and the truth, and the life."* We might capitalize that and quote him as saying *"I am The Way,"* for it did indeed become a name that the early church used. *"The Way,"* η οδος, adds to 352. It is one of the numbers of his name.

JESUS CHRIST: THE NUMBER OF HIS NAME

It is not coincidence that the gematria for the name Mary, *Μαριας,* is also 352. She had traveled to the one spot on this earth that bore his number by both its latitude and its longitude, and by its Golden Rectangle. And, without delay, as soon as she arrived in the ordained place, she gave birth to Jesus, the child who would become *"the Light of the world." "Light,"* λαμπας, adds to 352.

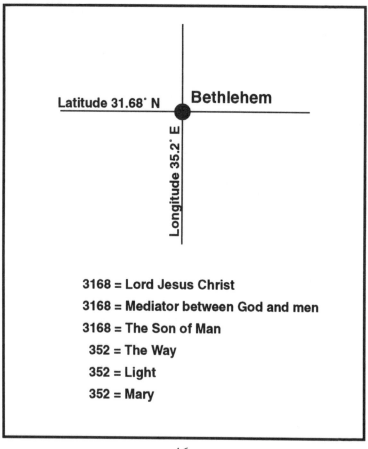

Latitude 31.68° N   ● **Bethlehem**

Longitude 35.2° E

3168 = Lord Jesus Christ
3168 = Mediator between God and men
3168 = The Son of Man
352 = The Way
352 = Light
352 = Mary

While noting this relationship of the Golden Rectangle as placed upon the equatorial and polar diameters of the earth, let's digress for just a moment to look at another rectangle that can be placed on these same meridians. I will show both in hopes that the comparison can be made easily.

The ancient mathematician, Pythagoras, has left his legacy of the single most important theorem in the whole of mathematics–the concept of the 3:4:5 right triangle. It is simply that $a^2 + b^2 = c^2$. Every school girl or boy learns this at the beginning of geometry class. In actuality, what Pythagoras has left for us is a theorem that establishes a fundamental characterization of time and space, and the laws that bind the universe. Pythagoras found a great truth!

It is not surprising that when we draw a 3:4:5 triangle on the polar and equatorial diameters of the earth, the long side of that triangle would be 3,168 miles. It bears the name of the Lord Jesus Christ.

We have just observed that a Golden Rectangle drawn on the polar and equatorial diameters of the earth has a long side of 3,368 miles, which is the gematria for the name Lord Jesus Christ also.

It is nothing short of fantastic that these two mathematical wonders–the Pythagorean 3:4:5 triangle, and the Golden Rectangle–when drawn on the diameter of the earth, reveal the name Lord Jesus Christ by both of its spellings. It carries us far beyond the realm of coincidence, and puts us into the realm of a divine Architect.

47

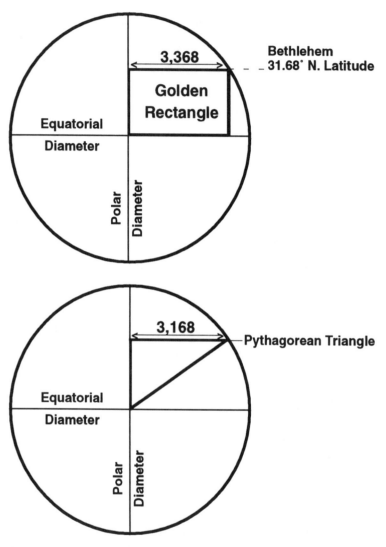

3368 = Lord Jesus Christ, *Κυριου Ιησους Χριστος*
3168 = Lord Jesus Christ, *Κυριος Ιησους Χριστος*

(Both the rectangle and the triangle are based upon the mean radius of the earth.)

JESUS CHRIST AND THE GOLDEN PROPORTION

The Golden Proportion has often been called the Divine Proportion, because it so beautifully shows the harmony in all nature. Plato called it the most binding of all mathematical relations, and the key to the physics of the cosmos. It is the relationship of Unity to creation.

The first act of creation was the *"breaking forth of light,"* בשחר, which by gematria is 528. This first creative act was the division of Unity, but a very special kind of division, in which 1 (Unity) can be expressed in two terms. In geometry, this occurs only when the smaller term is to the larger term as the larger term is to the smaller plus the larger. This may sound confusing, but it can be illustrated very simply.

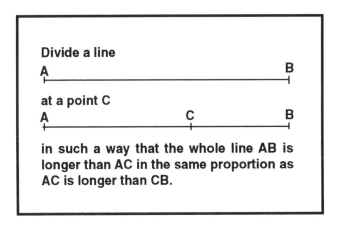

Divide a line

A _____ B

at a point C

A _____ C _____ B

in such a way that the whole line AB is longer than AC in the same proportion as AC is longer than CB.

Thus when Unity is divided, that which is separated becomes part of the whole. The ratio is 1:1.618. In mathematics, the Greek letter ϕ (pronounced phi) is used as a symbol of this proportion. It describes the most intimate

relationship that the created can have with the Creator–
the primal or first division of One.

"The breaking forth of light," בשחר, bears the number
528 by its gematria. Let's draw a square whose perimeter
is 528. It will have sides of 132.

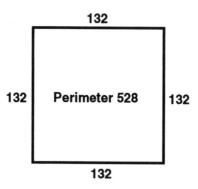

Next, let's project the Golden Proportion of this square.
Mathematically this is done by multiplying 132 by .618, the
Golden Proportion. This will produce a Golden Rectangle.

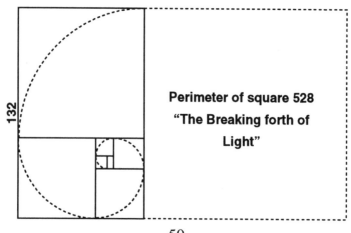

Each time we divide off the square within the rectangle, it leaves us with another Golden Rectangle. This can be done mathematically to infinity, but graphically it can only be portrayed about seven times and still be visible. Then connect the corners of the squares within the Golden Rectangle, and it will produce the Golden Spiral. It is the same spiral that can be seen in the seed pattern of most flowers, in the pine cone, the nautilus shell, the swirl of hair on the human head, and the grand spiral of the galaxy of the heavens.

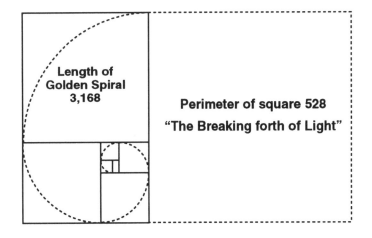

Length of Golden Spiral 3,168

Perimeter of square 528 "The Breaking forth of Light"

The relationship of the Golden Proportion to *"the break-ing forth of light"* is 3168, the name Lord Jesus Christ. He was indeed the Light of the World.

The place of his birth was identified by a latitude of 31.68° N. and a longitude of 35.2° E. If we drew another Golden Rectangle, and simply changed the dimensions, its relationship to Bethlehem would be astonishing.

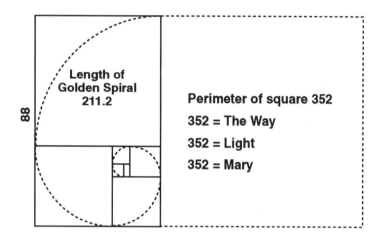

352 = Perimeter of square

352 = The Way (Jesus)

352 = Light (he was the light of the world)

352 = Mary

88 = Long side of Golden Rectangle

88 = A Child is born (Isaiah 9:6), ילד ילד

211.2 = Length of Golden Spiral

2112 = A virgin shall conceive and bear a Son and shall call his name Emmanuel (Isaiah 7:14),

העלמה הרה וילדת בן וקראת שמו עמנו אל

These relationships are startling, because they are the same relationships that occur when we consider the latitude of Bethlehem in relation to the circumference of the earth.

The latitude of Bethlehem is 31.68° N., which is 35.2% of the 90° between the equator and the pole. (90 x .352 = 31.68). That same latitude, when used as a percent of the entire 360 degrees of the circumference of the earth, is 8.8%. (360 x .088 = 31.68).

We have just seen the beautiful relationship of 352 and 88 to the Golden Proportion. It is thrilling to find it again in the dimensions of the earth. It was planted there by the divine Architect who placed the Number of His Name in Bethlehem, for he knew from the beginning that the Saviour of the world would be born there.

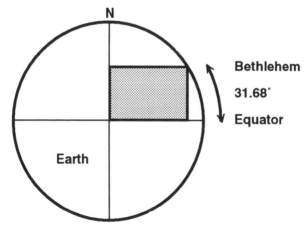

31.68° is 35.2% of distance from equator to pole
31.68° is 8.8% of distance around the world

Bethlehem was the assigned location for the promised ruler to come. God had prophesied by the hand of Micah that this tiny little middle east town would produce the most wonderful event that the world had ever seen.

> *"You, Bethlehem Ephratah, you who are little among the thousands of Judah, out of you shall He come forth to Me to be ruler in Israel, and His goings forth have been from of old, from the days of eternity."*
> (Micah 5:2)

The identification of the place of his birth bears an interesting number in its gematria.

1958 = You, Bethlehem Ephratah, you who are little

ואתה ביתלחם אפרתה צעיר

Again the Golden Proportion (.618034) tells us that this promised ruler that was to come out of Bethlehem is indeed the Lord Jesus Christ, for if we divide 1958 by ϕ the result is 3168. This tells us that a Golden Rectangle whose short side is 1958 will have a long side of 3168.

$$1958 \div .618034 = 3168$$

JESUS CHRIST AND THE GOLDEN PROPORTION

The prophet Isaiah wrote *"Therefore the Lord himself will give you a sign: The virgin will be with child and will give birth to a son, and will call him Immanuel."* (Isaiah 7:14) Matthew quoted this, and then told us what the name Immanuel means. He said, *"Behold, a virgin shall be with child, and shall bring forth a son, and they shall call his name Emmanuel, which being interpreted is, God with us."* (Matt. 1:23)

The relationship of this name to the Golden Proportion is interesting indeed. The meaning of the name – *"God with us"* in the Greek text adds to 1236, which is twice the Golden Proportion. (2 x 618 = 1236) Yet, the name Immanuel, as Isaiah wrote it, עמנו אל, adds to 197. The number 197 is the closest whole number that can be used as the diameter of a circle whose circumference is 618.

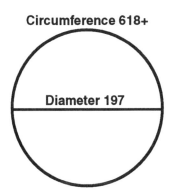

Circumference 618+

Diameter 197

But the relationship of Immanuel to the Golden Proportion is just beginning. From here it grows and blossoms into a thing of magnificent beauty.

The meaning of Immanuel is *"God with us."* It bears the number 1236, or twice the Golden Proportion. Jesus, in his role as The Branch, was said to be the branch that would grow out of the root of David. Isaiah calls him *"A Root out of dry ground."*

1236 = God with us, μεθ ημων θεος
1236 = A Root out of dry ground, שרש מארץ ציה

The ground was indeed dry, for the dynasty of David seemingly ended, and for long years they have lamented the loss of their kingdom and their glorious Temple. But the ground was not completely dry, for the root sprouted again. The Branch will grow into a glorious tree, that will fill the whole earth with its life and peace.

This glorious work of The Branch was foretold long ago by faithful Jacob. When Jacob was old, and knew that he would soon die, *"he called unto his twelve sons, and said, Gather yourselves together, that I may tell you that which shall befall you in the last days."* (Genesis 49:1)

Note that Jacob was pointing all the way down through time to the *"last days."*

To his son Judah he said:

> *"Judah is a lion's whelp; my son, you have gone up from the prey; he stoops, he crouches like a lion; and like a lioness, who can rouse him up? The sceptre shall not*

depart from Judah, nor the lawmaker from between his feet, until Shiloh come, and the gathering of the people shall be to him. Binding his foal to the vine and his ass's colt to the choice vine, he washes his clothing in wine, and his raiment in the blood of grapes. His eyes shall be dark from wine, and his teeth white from milk."

The translation somewhat obscures the meaning in places. It makes more sense in Hebrew; however, some parts of it are obvious. It is a prophecy of the coming of Jesus as the *"Lion of the tribe of Judah"* and as Shiloh, the peacemaker. The portion dealing with the sceptre is replete with the Golden Proportion.

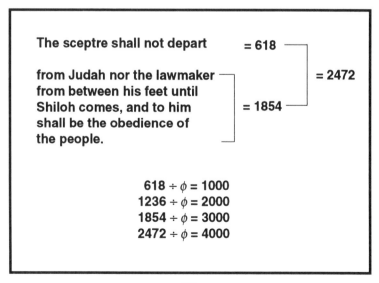

The sceptre shall not depart = 618 ⌐
from Judah nor the lawmaker ⌐ = 2472
from between his feet until
Shiloh comes, and to him = 1854 ⌐
shall be the obedience of
the people.

$$618 \div \phi = 1000$$
$$1236 \div \phi = 2000$$
$$1854 \div \phi = 3000$$
$$2472 \div \phi = 4000$$

The prophecy is talking about rulership. The first king to come from the line of Judah was King David. His kingdom was a type of the reign of King Jesus, the Lion of the Tribe of Judah, who is of the lineage of Judah through David.

Speaking of the time when Jesus would return and take his role of King, the prophet Zechariah said, *"The Lord shall be king over all the earth."* It adds to 618, the Golden Proportion.

Malachi also spoke of that coming day, and he asked the question, *"Who can endure the day of his coming? Who can stand at his appearing?"* The Hebrew word for *"his appearing"* is הראותו, and its letter-numbers add to 618.

The ninth chapter of the book of Daniel contains a prophecy regarding the time of the coming of Jesus, both as the Messiah whom they would kill, and as the King who will reign. The prophecy speaks of six things that would occur before all this could be accomplished.

1. *to finish transgression*
2. *to put an end to sin*
3. *to atone for wickedness*
4. *to bring in everlasting righteousness*
5. *to seal up vision and prophecy*
6. *to anoint the Most Holy*

The first three of these were accomplished when he died

on the cross. The remaining three have not yet happened, but will be accomplished at the time of his return.

618 = to seal up vision and prophecy
2 x 618 = 1236 = to anoint the Most Holy

The prophet Zechariah, when speaking of the time of Jesus' return, told of the world-wide nature of his kingship. He wrote, *"The Lord shall be king over all the earth."* (Zechariah 14:9) The letter-numbers of the text add to 618.

Noting the uses of 618 and its multiples and their relationship to the return of Jesus as King, perhaps it would not be too bold to speculate regarding the *time* of his return. As seen on page 57, the prophecy of the coming of Shiloh in Genesis 49:10 is divided into the Golden Proportion and its multiples, by even thousands. Many ancient writers have suggested that there would be 3,000 years from Adam to King David, and another 3,000 years from King David to the "King Messiah." And we know from history that there were 1,000 years between the time when David was anointed king over all Israel, and moved his seat of government to Jerusalem, to the time when Jesus was born. Can we project this and say that there will be 2,000 more years from Jesus' birth to his return as King? If so, then the prophecy of the coming of Shiloh in Genesis 49:10 can be seen to show these thousand-year periods.

Another interesting use of the Golden Proportion and

its relation to the coming of Jesus as King can be seen in the prophecy of Isaiah which we have already quoted: *"A Shoot proceeds from the stump of Jesse and a Branch out of his roots."* (Isaiah 11:1)

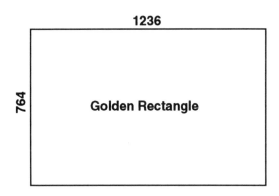

1236
764
Golden Rectangle

1236 = a Root out of dry ground (Isaiah 53:2)
764 = a Shoot proceeds from the stump of Jesse (Isaiah 11:1)

The tender Shoot that came from the stump of Jesse was born as a baby in Bethlehem. He grew to be the man Christ Jesus who presented himself as man's redeemer, to heal us from the death sentence placed upon Adam. It was, as Isaiah prophesied, *"By His wounds we are healed"* (Isaiah 53:5) He is the personification of the Golden Proportion.

618 = By His wounds, בחברתו

6
Jesus Christ and the Magnificent Math

Jesus not only told his disciples that he must go away, but that he would also return. Nearly 2,000 years have passed, and his disciples are still awaiting that glorious return. Every generation since his ascension has eagerly hoped that he would return in their time.

When he left that little band of followers on the Mount of Olives, and ascended up into the clouds out of their sight, two angels stood there with them, and said:

> *"Men of Galilee, why do you stand here looking into the sky? This same Jesus, who has been taken from you into heaven, will come back in the same way you have seen him go into heaven."*

The prophecies indicate that when he returns he will be the one to fulfill the promise of a king to sit on David's throne, forever. He is said to be the one who holds the key to the house of David. Isaiah talked about that key, he said: *"I will place on his shoulder the key to the house of David; what he opens no one can shut, and what he shuts no one can open."* And we know it was prophetic of Jesus because Jesus, himself, quoted this to John when he gave him the Revelation, and applied it to himself.

Revelation 3:7. *"These are the words of him who is holy and true, who holds the key of David. What he opens no one can shut, and what he shuts no one can open."* Yes, Jesus, indeed, holds the key to the house of David–the dynasty that was promised to last forever. But what is the key?

Not surprisingly, we find the answer in the Golden Proportion and its beautiful Golden Spiral.

The key that Isaiah spoke of is the word מפתח, which has a number value of 528. It is the same number that we have seen for *"The breaking forth of light."* Its use with the Golden Proportion is beautiful! It identifies the King as being the Lord Jesus Christ, it speaks of his work of overthrowing the present evil order, and of his setting up his kingdom of righteousness in the earth.

The Golden Spiral is found throughout nature in its reproductive process. The embryos of all vertebrates (including man) begin in the shape of the Golden Spiral. It is a fundamental principle of reproduction and growth. When King Jesus uses the key to unlock and open the access to the throne of David, that kingdom will grow to fill the whole earth.

When Daniel interpreted Nebuchadnezzar's dream of the great image, representing man's governments, he told of a small stone that was cut out of the mountain without hands. This small stone smote the great image on its feet and the whole thing crumbled and was ground to powder and the wind blew it away. Then the stone began to grow, and it grew so much that it eventually filled the whole earth. (Daniel 2)

He was describing the growth of the long-promised Kingdom of the antitypical David, King Jesus. It all starts with a small stone. But that stone began to grow just like the Golden Spiral, in logarithmic proportions, and will become earth commensurate.

This can be shown graphically by a square whose perimeter is 528, and whose Golden Rectangle has a long side of 132 with an inscribed Golden Spiral of 316.8.

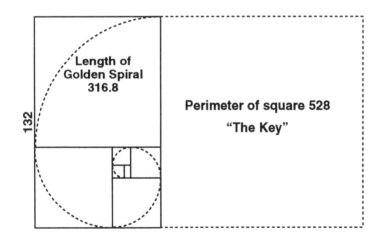

528 = The Key
528 = The Breaking forth of Light
1320 = The stone cut out of the mountain
132 = The Kingdom is the Lord's
3168 = Lord Jesus Christ

What happens when the stone grows? I would like to illustrate it graphically, but this page is too small, in fact, it will not fit into this room, or into this state, or even this nation – it keeps on growing until it fills the whole world. However, it can be represented mathematically.

"The Stone cut out of the mountain" has a number value of 1320. Let's make it grow by dividing by the Golden Proportion: 1320 ÷ .618 = 2136. This number is the gematria for a description of Jesus in his role as King of Kings and Lord of Lords. The Apostle Paul called him *"The blessed and only ruler."* (I Tim. 6:15) It adds to 2136. But let's divide again by the Golden Proportion: 2136 ÷ .618 = 3456. This number describes him as ruler in his great Kingdom.

3456 = Alpha and Omega, the beginning and the end.

αλφα και το Ω η αρχη και το τελος, (Rev. 1:8)

3456 = The marriage of the Bride and the Lamb

ο γαμος του αρνιου και η γυνη αυτου, (Rev. 19:7)

But gematria has another function as well as addition – the letter numbers can also be multiplied. By multiplication we get the following beautiful descriptions:

3456 = His Kingdom, מלכותו, (Psalm 145:13)

3456 = His dominion, ממשלתו, (Psalm 103:22)

3456 = His throne in the heavens,

בשמים הכין כסאו, (Psalm 103:19)

JESUS CHRIST AND THE MAGNIFICENT MATH

The Golden Proportion is sometimes called the Divine Proportion because it so beautifully displays the principle of the growth process–the process of creation. And, by extension, it also tells of the One of whom John said, *"All things were made by him, and without him was nothing made."*

The name Lord Jesus Christ, as has been shown, adds to 3168 (and sometimes to 3368). The name Jesus, *Ιησους*, adds to 888; and Christ, *Χριστος*, adds to 1480. There were many other names, titles, and phrases used in the Bible to identify him. There appears to be a pattern in the number equivalents for these names. Most of them are multiples of 37. The number 37 is a prime, and from it we get the name Jesus (24 x 37 = 888) and Christ (40 x 37 = 1480). In Appendix II will be found nearly 200 such names or phrases, all multiples of 37. I do not list them here because it would digress too much from the subject at hand. But this observation clearly shows an intended pattern.

Let's consider for a moment the name Jesus Christ and its prime root, 37. If we draw a square whose perimeter is 1480 (Christ), and project its Golden Rectangle, the long side of the rectangle will be 370, and the Golden Spiral that can be traced within it will have a length of 888. It hardly seems to be a coincidence. His name, and its root, are part of the whole pattern of creation, involving the growth principle of the Golden Proportion–the Divine Proportion. It suggests that the numbers of his name have been planted in all of his works.

65

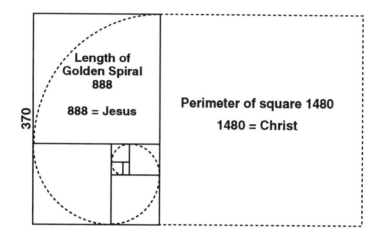

Let's look, for a moment, at some of the uses in the scriptures of the numbers involved in this Golden Rectangle. I call it Magnificent Math!

1480 = Christ, Χριστος

1480 = Son of God, υιος Κυριος

1480 = His Kingdom, βασιλειαν αυτου

148 = Passover, פסח (Jesus was the antitypical Passover Lamb)

148 = Blood, נצח (It is through His shed blood that we have redemption)

888 = Jesus, Ιησους

888 = I am the Life, ειμι η ζωη

888 = The light dwells in Him, ונהירא עמה שרא

888 = A priest with Urim and Thumim (prophetic of Jesus), כהן לאורים ולתמים (Ezra 2:63)

888 = Salvation of our God, ישועת אלהינו (Isaiah 52:10)

370 = My Messiah, במשיחי

370 =Stump, עקר (Jesus was the Branch from the Stump of Jesse.)

37 = Only Begotten, יחידה, (Jesus was the Only Begotten son of God.)

37 = Only Son, היחיד

370 = He reigns, משל

370 = The Breaker, פרץ, (Micah 2:13 uses this name to represent Jesus. It is the name of the constellation that pictures his return.)

It is no coincidence that the names Messiah and Christ are linked together, 4 x 370 = 1480. They both mean the same thing – *anointed.* And it was Jesus, whose number is 888 that was the promised *anointed* one, the Messiah, the Christ. That these three primary names by which he is known should come together in the same Golden Rectangle and Golden Spiral is thrilling. It surely is Magnificent Math!

But, as if this were not sufficiently staggering to the awareness, we can simply double the above numbers and again find the same abundant evidence that it was part of a great mathematical plan. In this one it depicts Jesus as the maker of all things, just as John said, *"Without him was nothing made that was made."* It also depicts him as the *"root and offspring of David"* and as the *"Son of Man,"* the *"only begotten"* of the Father, and the *"river of life"* to all mankind. The numbers are all multiples of 37.

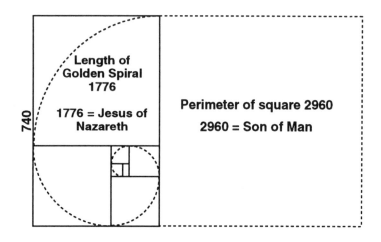

2960 = Son of Man, $\upsilon\iota o\varsigma\ \tau o\upsilon\ \alpha\nu\theta\rho\omega\pi o\upsilon$

296 = Only begotten, $\mu o\nu o\gamma\varepsilon\nu\eta$

296 = The beautiful Branch of Jehovah, צֶמַח יְהוָה לִצְבִי
(Isaiah 4:2)

1776 = Jesus of Nazareth, $I\eta\sigma o\upsilon\ N\alpha\zeta\omega\rho\alpha\iota o\nu^{\jmath}$

1776 = Lord of the Sabbath, $\kappa\upsilon\rho\iota o\varsigma\ \sigma\alpha\beta\beta\alpha\tau o\upsilon$

1776 = River of life, $\pi o\tau\alpha\mu o\varsigma\ \zeta\omega\eta\varsigma$ (Rev. 22:1)

1776 = I am the Root and Offspring of David,
        $\varepsilon\gamma\omega\ \varepsilon\iota\mu\iota\ \eta\ \rho\iota\zeta\alpha\ \kappa\alpha\iota\ \gamma\varepsilon\nu o\varsigma\ \Delta\alpha\upsilon\iota\delta^{\jmath}$ (Rev. 22:16)

740 = Creation, $\kappa\tau\iota\sigma\iota\varsigma$

740 = You have laid the foundation of the earth,
        הארין יסדת (Psalm 102:25)

740 = Blood of Jesus, $\alpha\iota\mu\alpha\ I\eta\sigma o\upsilon,$ (I John 1:7)

---

1   In gematria, one unit, known as *colel,* may be added or subtracted
from the value of any word without affecting the meaning.

JESUS CHRIST AND THE MAGNIFICENT MATH

Another interesting use of the number 1776 (a multiple of 37) is found in Genesis regarding the first act of creation. *"And God said let there be light, and there was light; and God saw the light that it was good,"* האור כיטוב ויאמר אלהים יהי אור ויהי אור וירא אלהים את, which adds to 1776,(Genesis 1:3). When this number is used as the perimeter of the square, the Golden Rectangle that can be projected has a length of 444 and the Golden Spiral that can be inscribed within it has a length of 1065.6. These numbers span the entire scope of time from creation to the competed work of God – the New Jerusalem that comes down and engulfs the whole earth. Let me share with you the Magnificent Math!

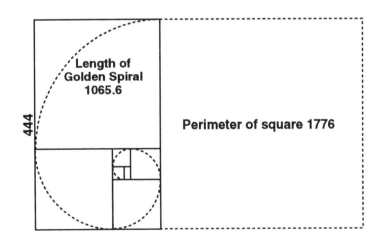

Length of Golden Spiral 1065.6

444

Perimeter of square 1776

JESUS CHRIST: THE NUMBER OF HIS NAME

First we'll drop the decimal points because they mean nothing in gematria. This number, 1776, is the gematria for the beautiful completed work of God in bringing Israel and all nations into this promised Davidic kingdom that will last forever.

1776 = And they shall call you The City of God, the Zion
of the Holy One of Israel. (Isaiah 60:14)
וקראו לך עיר יהוה ציון קדוש ישראל

There is, however, another aspect of the City of God that is described in Revelation as the New Jerusalem that comes down out of heaven. The picture is of a glorious kingdom that comes down and engulfs the whole earth in one harmonious whole, both heavenly and earthly. The Apostle John described this New Jerusalem as The Bride, the completed company of the saints of God, who receive their new married name. *"And I will write on him the name of my God, and the name of the City of my God, the New Jerusalem,"* (Rev. 3:12). The gematria of the text is precisely the length of the Golden Spiral in the above Golden Rectangle, 10656.

10656 = And I will write on him the name of my God, and
the name of the City of my God, the New Jerusalem, *και γραψωεπ αυτον το ονομα του Θεου μου και το ονομα της πολεως του Θεου μου της καινης Ιερουσαλημ.*

"Come, I will show you the bride, the wife of the Lamb. And he carried me away in the spirit to a mountain great and high, and showed me the Holy City, Jerusalem, coming down out of heaven from God. It shone with the glory of God, and its brilliance was like that of a very precious jewel, like a jasper, clear as crystal. It had a great, high wall with twelve gates, and with twelve angels at the gates. On the gates were written the names of the twelve tribes of Israel. There were three gates on the east, three on the north, three on the south and three on the west. The wall of the city had twelve foundations and on them were the names of the twelve apostles of the Lamb."
(Revelation 21:9-14)

Thus the city is described as having twelve gates, bearing the names of the twelve tribes of Israel. And it had twelve foundations, bearing the names of the twelve apostles. In Revelation 7 is described a Lamb standing on Mount Zion and with him were 12,000 from each of the tribes of Israel. When we add the gematria for the names of the twelve tribes listed there, and multiply by 12,000, the total becomes 10,656. And when we add the gematria for the names of the twelve apostles, they also total 10,656. It carries us far beyond the possibility of coincidence. That number was planned from the beginning to represent the completed work of God.

The names of the twelve tribes of Israel, as listed in Revelation 7, are as follows:

Tribe	Greek	Number
Judah	Ιουδα	485
Reuben	Ρουβην	630
Gad	Γαδ	8
Asher	Ασηρ	309
Nepthalim	Νεφθαλειμ	650
Manasses	Μανασσησ	700
Simeon	Συμεων	1495
Levi	Λευι	445
Issachar	Ισσαχαρ	1112
Zebulon	Ζαβουλων	1360
Joseph	Ιωσηφ	1518
Benjamin	Βενιαμιν	168
		8880

8,880 x 12,000 from each tribe = 106,560,000
Dropping the zeros: 888 x 12 = 10656

There has been no "cutting and fitting" to make the numbers work. The names, as shown above are the way in which they are spelled in a *Thayer Greek Lexicon*. The total, 10656 represents the completed work of God, the New Jerusalem coming down out of heaven from God, and engulfing the whole world.

JESUS CHRIST AND THE MAGNIFICENT MATH

The city not only had twelve gates, bearing the names of the twelve tribes of Israel, just like Ezekiel's city, but it also had twelve foundations, bearing the names of the twelve apostles. The gematria of their names also adds to 10656. This amazing fact carries us far beyond the realm of coincidence and into the realm of the magnificent works of God.

Peter	$\Pi\varepsilon\tau\rho\varsigma$	755
Andrew	$A\nu\delta\rho\varepsilon\alpha\varsigma$	361
James	$I\alpha\kappa\omega\beta\varsigma$	1103
John	$I\omega\alpha\nu\nu\eta\varsigma$	1119
Philip	$\Phi\iota\lambda\iota\pi\pi\varsigma$	980
Nathanael	$N\alpha\theta\alpha\nu\alpha\eta\lambda$	150
Levi (Matthew)	$\Lambda\varepsilon\upsilon\iota$	445
Thomas	$\Theta\omega\mu\alpha\varsigma$	1050
James (son of Alpheus)	$I\alpha\kappa\omega\beta\varsigma\ A\lambda\phi\alpha\iota\upsilon$	2115
Labbaeus (Thaddeus)	$\Lambda\varepsilon\beta\beta\alpha\iota\varsigma$	320
Simon the Canannite	$\Sigma\iota\mu\omega\nu\ \upsilon\ \kappa\alpha\nu\alpha\nu\alpha\iota\varsigma$	1573
Judas	$I\upsilon\delta\alpha\varsigma$	685
		10656

When we add the sum of the digits it becomes 18. (1 + 6 + 5 + 6 = 18) The numbers 1 and 8 are basic to an understanding of Biblical gematria. The number 1 always denotes a beginning; and the number 8 is representative of a new beginning. It is built upon the principle of the octave. The numbers 1 through 7 are the scale of tones, followed by the 8th, the same note as 1 but 7 tones higher. This is repeated over and over in the many tones of the musical scale. The number 1 is the beginning, and the number 8 is the new beginning. Thus, in observing that the number for the completed works of God, 10656, resolves to 18, we see the reality of the beginning and the new beginning. It is shown in the time features of his work of creation and his plan for man.

The six creation days were followed by a seventh, in which God rested from his works of creation. These in turn are followed by the great 8th day, which begins a time called eternity. Or the same analogy can be made with the seventh day. It is divided into seven periods of 1,000 years each – the last of which is the long promised Earth's Great Millennium. At the completion of the 7,000 years the beautiful description of the New Jerusalem will come down from God and encompass the whole world with its life and peace – it is the time of the New Beginning, the great 8th day.

In the gematria of the Bible, the number 1 is used as representing God and the beginning work of creation. The number 8 is used as representing Jesus Christ and the work of the New Beginning. It is through the atoning blood of Jesus, whose number is 888, that a new beginning for man was promised. The number 18 is often used for the combined concept of the Deity and the work of creation and redemption. And, as is the case with gematria, sometimes zeros are placed in the number, but it does not change the basic meaning of the number. Thus it is observed that the numbers 108, 1080 and 1008 still retain the same meaning.

When Jesus said *"I am the Alpha and the Omega, the First and the Last, the Beginning and the End,"* (Revelation 22:13), he was not only making reference to the first and last letters of the Greek alphabet, but he was also saying "I am the 1 and the 8," for Alpha is 1 and Omega is 800.

Here are some of the uses of 1 and 8 in the gematria of the scriptures. Their reference to Jehovah and to Jesus Christ, and to beginnings, speaks for itself.

1000 = Lord, $Kυριου$

800 = Lord, $Kυριος$

100 = The Most High, על

111 = The Most High, עליא

111 = Wonderful, אלפ (the prophetic name given to Jesus in Isaiah 9:6)

1101 = The Creator of the ends of the earth, בורא קצות הארץ, (Isaiah 40:28)

8 = Beginning, או

8 = Entrance, באה

888 = Jesus, $Iησους$

888 = I am the life, $ειμι$ $η$ $ζωη$

8888 = He must reign until he has put all enemies under his feet (I Cor. 15:25) (When this is accomplished, then comes the New Beginning, the great 8th day.)

JESUS CHRIST: THE NUMBER OF HIS NAME

When the 1 and the 8 are combined we get 18, 108, 1080, 1008, 10080. Here are some examples from the gematria of the Bible.

180 = Maker, פעל (A title often used of the Creator)

18 = He who lives, חי (Referring to Jehovah, Dan. 12:7)

1080 = The Holy Spirit, $\pi\nu\varepsilon\nu\mu\alpha$ τo $\alpha\gamma\iota o\nu$

1080 = God himself who formed the earth and made it,
הוא האלהים יצר הארץ ועשה (Isaiah 45:18)

1080 = Heaven is my throne and the earth is my footstool, (Isaiah 66:1)

1008 = The work of thy fingers, מעשה אצבעתיך, (referring to the works of creation, Psalm 8:3)

1008 = The Lord is high above all nations, and His glory above the heavens, בהיכל קדשו הם מפניו כל הארץ יהוה (Psalm 113:4)

10080 = He shall be great, and shall be called the Son of the Highest, and the Lord God shall give Him the throne of David, $o\nu\tau o\varsigma$ $\varepsilon\sigma\tau\alpha\iota$ $\mu\varepsilon\gamma\alpha\varsigma$ $\kappa\alpha\iota$ $\nu\iota o\varsigma$ $\nu\psi\iota\sigma\tau o\nu$ $\kappa\lambda\eta\theta\eta\sigma\varepsilon\tau\alpha\iota$ $\kappa\alpha\iota$ $\delta\omega\sigma\varepsilon\iota$ $\alpha\nu\tau\omega$ $\kappa\nu\rho\iota o\varsigma$ o $\Theta\varepsilon o\varsigma$ $\tau o\nu$ $\theta\rho o\nu o\nu$ $\Delta\alpha\nu\iota\delta,$ (Luke 1:32)

The 1 and the 8 are not only basic to the Creator, they are also basic to the concept of creation, and they are planted in the geometry of our Solar System. The use of multiples of 108 in the dimensions of the earth, sun and moon are startling. It gives evidence of a master plan by a Master Mathematician. Let's look at its Magnificent Math.

$$2 \times 108 = 216$$
$$4 \times 108 = 432$$
$$8 \times 108 = 864$$

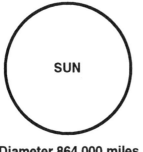

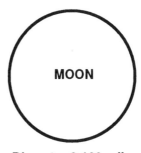

Diameter 864,000 miles
Radius 432,000 miles

Diameter 2,160 miles
Radius 1,080 miles

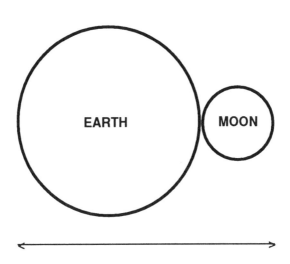

The Earth-Moon unit has a combined
diameter of 10,080 miles.

The basic element of all creation is Hydrogen. It is the lightest of all the elements. It bears the Atomic Number 1, and the Atomic Weight of 1.0080 – this element which is basic to all creation bears the numbers 1 and 8. Of all the cosmic matter in the Universe, 92% is pure Hydrogen. All of the other elements were formed from the fusion of Hydrogen, giving it additional protons and electrons. But the complete periodic table of the elements begins with Hydrogen. It is the fundamental element of creation. It is thrilling to realize that the Creator planted his numbers in all of his creation– the numbers 1 and 8, the beginning and the new beginning.

In Revelation 21 and 22 we find a description of that new beginning, the great 8th day. It describes the Holy City, the New Jerusalem, descending from God and encompassing the whole earth. We have seen how its dimensions, stated in feet, are commensurate with the dimensions of our earth. However, if we use the dimensions in furlongs, as is given in Revelation, it takes on added beauty and meaning.

The city is said to be a cube with sides of 12,000 furlongs. This would make the square measure of each side 144,000 furlongs. A cube has six sides, thus 6 x 144,000 = 864,000 furlongs. It is commensurate with the diameter of the sun.

When Jesus made reference to that completed Kingdom of God that is represented by the New Jerusalem, he said, *"Then shall the righteous shine forth as the sun in the kingdom of their Father."* It is not a coincidence that the dimensions of the New Jerusalem bear the solar number, 864,000, or that the name Jerusalem, *Ιερουσαλημ,* adds to 864. Those who *"shine forth in the kingdom of their Father"* are called, in Revelation, *"saints."* The gematria for *"saints," αγιων,* is 864.

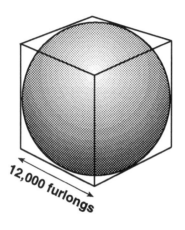

The New Jerusalem
12,000 furlongs each side
144,000 square furlongs each side
864,000 square furlongs in surface of cube
864,000 miles diameter of the sun
864 = Jerusalem
864 = Saints
864 = God, *Θεων*

We have observed that the New Jerusalem is commensurate with the earth, seeming to engulf and surround it;

now the above diagram shows it to be commensurate with the sun also. If we were to draw a square around the sun, its perimeter would measure 3,456,000 miles. The name of the New Jerusalem – *The City of my God* (Rev. 3:12) – has the number equivalent of 3456. It is numerically describing its relation to the sun, the source of light and life for all living things on this earth. And again, the sum of the digits reverts back to the basic 1 and 8 (3 + 4 + 5 + 6 = 18).

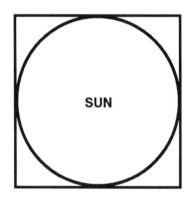

3,456,000 miles, perimeter of square
3456 = The City of my God (Rev. 3:12)

The sun and the moon are used repeatedly in the Bible as symbols. In the first chapter of Genesis we are told that they were to be not only for day and night, but also for "signs." The geometry of those orbs is so interwoven with the gematria of the scriptures that the intent of the Creator is apparent.

JESUS CHRIST AND THE MAGNIFICENT MATH

The story of redemption through the Lord Jesus Christ is not only told through the sun and moon, it is also told through the Zodiac. More than a hundred years ago a pastor of a church in Philadelphia, Pennsylvania, by the name of Joseph A. Seiss published a most revealing work describing the whole plan of God for the salvation of man as is illustrated in the signs of the Zodiac. The book has been republished in recent years by Kregel Publications. It is called *Gospel in the Stars.* The story that is told by these signs covers the whole span of time from man's beginning, his subsequent fall, his need of redemption, the suffering redeemer, the call and development of the church, the return of the Lord, the conquering of Satan, all the way to the complete ingathering of all mankind into the Kingdom of God.

The complete span of time that it takes the sun to pass through each of the 12 signs of the Zodiac is 25,920 years. Thus, seeing these signs as the progressive events in the history and future of man, 25,920 would represent the whole of the Plan of God for man's salvation.

It is exciting to realize that the Golden Proportion beautifully shows this relationship of the numbers of creation, to the numbers of the Redeemer, the Branch out of the root of David, and the number that represents the whole Plan of God – 25,920. The Magnificent Math covers the whole scope of that glorious Plan!

Let's draw a square whose perimeter is 432 – the number that is commensurate with the radius of the sun. It is, in fact, one of the numbers assigned to The Branch. Then we'll extend its Golden Proportion and inscribe its Golden Spiral.

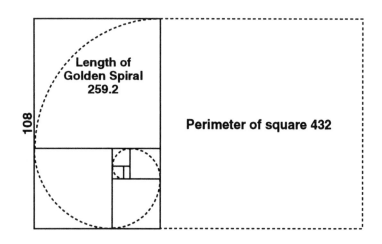

432 = The Branch of Jehovah, צמח יהוה (by multiplication) (Isaiah 4:2)

108 = He was pierced, מחלל (Isaiah 53:5) (Prophetic of Jesus on the cross when they pierced his side and the blood spilled out onto the ground.)

108 = Red, חכלילי, (The color of his blood, the color of redemption.)

25,920 is the number of years required for the sun to make one complete circuit through the Zodiac. Both the sum of its digits and the product of its digits are 18.

$$2 \times 5 \times 9 \times 2 = 180$$
$$2 + 5 + 9 + 2 = 18$$

This brings us back to the prophecy/blessing that Jacob gave to his son Judah in Genesis 49.

> *"Judah is a lion's whelp; my son, you have gone up from the prey; he stoops, he crouches like a lion; and like a lioness, who can rouse him up? The sceptre shall not depart from Judah, nor a lawmaker from between his feet, until Shiloh comes, and the gathering of the people shall be to him. Binding his foal to the vine and his ass's colt to the choice vine, he washes his clothing in wine, and his raiment in the blood of grapes. His eyes shall be dark from wine, and his teeth white from milk."* (Genesis 49: 9-12 from the King James II Version)

The identification of the lion is obvious. Revelation 5:5 identifies the Lion of Judah with the Root of David and the Lamb of God–it is Jesus. The gematria of the lion also identifies him with his position as king.

216 = Judah is a lion's whelp, גור אריה יהודה, (by multiplication, dropping the zeros)

216 = Lion, אריה

216 = power, גבורה

216 = All nations shall serve him, כל גוים יעבדוהי, (Psalm 72:11

83

216 = The blood of grapes, דם ענבים, (Gen. 49:11)

216 = His dominion, משלו, (Zechariah 9:10, by multiplication)

2,160 miles in the diameter of the moon

2,160 years in each division of the Zodiac

Jacob's final words to Judah seem a bit confusing. *"His eyes shall be dark from wine and his teeth white from milk."* The translation obscures the meaning. The Hebrew word here translated *"dark"* has the meaning of *"sparkling red."* The addition of its letter-numbers totals 108.

108 = sparkling red, חכלילי (216 ÷ 2 = 108)

The *"sparkling red"* of his eyes and the white of his teeth is another way of saying what Isaiah 1:18 is describing: *"Though your sins be as scarlet, they shall be white as snow; though they are red as crimson, they shall be like wool."*

108 = They shall be white, ילבינו

The *"red"* of original sin is canceled out by the *"red"* of Jesus' blood, leaving white. Notice that the *"sparkling red"* and the *"they shall be white"* both bear the same number, 108. It is because he canceled the redness of sin with the redness of his blood when *"he was pierced,"* (108), that he will be given the throne of David, and will bring in everlasting righteousness, symbolized by white.

In the number symbology of the scriptures, 1 means "beginning," and 8 means "new beginning," and both are embodied in the work of Jesus–the work of creation, redemption, and restoration.

108 = He was pierced, מחלל, (Isaiah 53:5)

10080 = He shall be great, and shall be called Son of the Highest, and the Lord God shall give Him the throne of David, (Luke 1:32)

Red, 108, is canceled out by red, 108, leaving white. I was made vividly aware of this one day when I entered a photofinishers darkroom. The only light in a darkroom is red. That day I was wearing a white shirt with red spots on it. As I entered the darkroom, all the red spots suddenly disappeared, and my shirt was totally white. The red light had canceled out my red spots. My thoughts immediately went to the beautiful ransom sacrifice of Jesus Christ, and my heart rejoiced to realize that he had canceled out the redness of my sin, and made me white in his sight.

Red, 108 on red, 108, produces 216. This canceling out of the redness of sin is accomplished by the *Lion,* 216; and when he is King on the throne of David, *"all nations will serve him,"* (216) when *"his dominion,"* (216) shall be to the ends of the earth. This marvelous addition of 108 + 108 = 216 was encoded into the scriptures by the sublime wisdom of God. It is part of his Magnificent Math!

At the time of the Exodus, when the Israelites left the bondage in Egypt and began their trek across the wilderness of Sinai, God called their leader, Moses, up into Mount Horeb, and there he gave him the Tables of the Law. When Moses came down from the mount, he read the Law to the people and they agreed to its terms. It was, in actuality, a marriage covenant between God and Israel. Israel said "I do" and entered into that marriage covenant when they replied, *"All these things will we do."* It is most interesting that the gematria for Horeb, חורב, is 216. That law covenant is represented by the moon in the symbology of the Bible, and the diameter of the moon is 2,160 miles. It was not a coincidence.

Moonlight is the reflected light of the sun. The sun represents the glorious light of the Gospel of Christ, and the New Covenant that was ushered in by Jesus as he hung on the cross of Calvary. The moon, 216, is the Old Law Covenant, and the sun, 864, is the New Covenant. This is pictured in Revelation 12:1:

> *"A great and wondrous sign appeared in heaven: a woman clothed with the sun, with the moon under her feet and a crown of twelve stars on her head."*

At the very hour in which Jesus died on the cross, 3:00 in the afternoon, the moon eclipsed. When the moon rose over Jerusalem that night, it was still eclipsed for 17 minutes. In actuality, the light from the sun had caused the shadow of the earth to obscure the light from the moon. In symbology, the light from the sun – New Covenant – superseded the light from the moon – Law Covenant. At the moment of his death, at 3:00 that afternoon, the old Law Covenant came to an end: the divorce was finalized.

The relationship of the solar number to the lunar number can be seen in the diagram below.

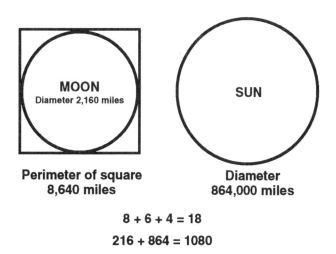

MOON
Diameter 2,160 miles

SUN

**Perimeter of square
8,640 miles**

**Diameter
864,000 miles**

8 + 6 + 4 = 18
216 + 864 = 1080

A few hours before they nailed Jesus to the cross, he condemned those who were the protectors of the Law, the Pharisees, and said, *"Your house is left unto you desolate."* They were to be no longer a married woman, but *"desolate,"* forsaken, and left without a protector-provider. The Apostle Paul said that when Jesus died, the Law Covenant died with him: *"He took it away, nailing it to his cross,"* (Col. 2:14). Within a few years their Temple was destroyed. The meeting place between Israel and God was gone. The place of atonement by animal sacrifices was gone. They were driven from their holy city and left desolate, to wander throughout the earth without a protector-provider.

But God will re-marry Israel, just as was prophesied in the book of Hosea.

> *"I will give back her vineyards and will make the Valley of Achor a door of hope. And she will answer there* (say "I do") *as in the days of her youth, as in the day she came up out of Egypt* (when she said "I do" at Horeb). *In that day, declares the Lord, you will call me My Husband.... In that day I will cut a covenant for them* (a new marriage covenant).... *I will betroth you to me forever; I will betroth you in righteousness and justice, in love and compassion. I will betroth you in faithfulness, and you will acknowledge the Lord."* (Hosea 2)

> *"For the Israelites will live many days without king or prince, without sacrifice or sacred stones, without ephod or idol. Afterward the Israelites will return and seek the Lord their God and David their King. They*

will come trembling to the Lord and to his
blessings in the last days." (Hosea 3)

Isaiah described the same event in unmistakable language.

"You no longer shall be called Forsaken;
nor shall your land any longer be called
Desolate; but you shall be called 'My
delight is in Her'; and your land shall be
married; for Jehovah delights in you and
your land shall be married." (Isaiah 62:40)

In the interim, between the divorce and the re-marriage, another bride is being selected – a bride for Christ. The light of the sun superseded the light of the moon. The sun represents the glorious light of the gospel of Christ, and the age in which he is selecting his bride. They bear the solar number, 864.

864 = Saints, $\alpha\gamma\iota\omega\nu$
864 = the flock of God, $\pi o\iota\mu\nu\iota o\nu\ \Theta\varepsilon o\upsilon$, (I Pet. 5:2)

The marriage of Christ and his church is described in Revelation 19:7, 8:

"Let us rejoice and be glad and give him
glory: For the wedding of the Lamb has
come, and his bride has made herself ready.

*Fine linen, bright and clean, was given to
her to wear. Fine linen stands for the righteousness of saints."*

After John saw this, the angel said to him:

*"Come, I will show you the bride, the wife
of the Lamb. And he carried me away in
the Spirit to a mountain great and high, and
showed me the Holy City, Jerusalem, coming down out of heaven from God."*

It becomes apparent that the bride of the Lamb is the
New Jerusalem that comes down and spreads its glory upon
the earth. The gematria for Jerusalem, $I\varepsilon\rho o\upsilon\sigma\alpha\lambda\eta\mu$, is
864, just as the gematria for saints is 864. They shall surely
shine forth as the sun, 864,000.

However, when the Hebrew letters in the name Jerusalem are multiplied, they become 432 (dropping the zeros).
It reveals the close relationship between the heavenly
Jerusalem and the earthly Jerusalem: the relationship
between the bride of Christ and the re-marriage of God to
Israel. The name Jerusalem in Hebrew is ירושלם, and it
adds to 586 and multiplies to 432. Note the interplay
between these numbers and the re-marriage of Israel.

That re-marriage is prophesied in Isaiah 62:4, and its
gematria is amazing. It was encoded into the text and tells
its beautiful story.

"For Zion's sake, I will not be silent; and for Jerusalem's sake, I will not rest; until her righteousness goes forth as brightness and her salvation as a burning torch. And nations shall see your righteousness, and all kings your glory; and you shall be called by a new name which the mouth of Jehovah shall designate. You also shall be a crown of beauty in the hand of Jehovah, and a royal diadem in the hand of your God. You no longer shall be called 'Forsaken'; nor shall your land any longer be called 'Desolate'; but you shall be called 'My delight is in Her'; and your land 'Married'; for Jehovah delights in you, and your land shall be married." (Isaiah 62:1-4)

When it says *"her righteousness goes forth as brightness, and her salvation as a burning torch,"* it is making reference to the sun, for her married name is the solar number. But, just as the diameter of the sun, 864,000 represents the saints, 864, and heavenly Jerusalem bears the number 864, so earthly Jerusalem is represented by the radius of the sun, 432,000, for when its Hebrew letters are multiplied, they are 432.

Some have suggested that the above text from Isaiah is talking about the heavenly bride, the bride of Christ. However, encoded into the text is evidence that it is prophetic of earthly Jerusalem. It was earthly Jerusalem that had been called "Desolate," and "Forsaken."

586 = Jerusalem, ירושלם
586 = You shall be called 'My delight is in her'
כי לך יקרא חפצי בה

432 = Jerusalem, ירושלם (multiplied)
432 = You shall be established in righteousness,
בצדקה תכונני, (Isaiah 54:14 multiplied)

Their king will be The Branch, who sits on the throne of David. His dynasty was promised to last forever. Isaiah called him *"The Branch of Jehovah, beautiful and glorious,"* and the letter-numbers of the text both add and multiply to 432. It is surely Magnificent Math!

7
Jesus Christ: The Star out of Jacob

There is a rather unusual story in the book of Numbers about a prophet of the Lord who had been offered money by a Gentile ruler to place a curse upon Israel. This prophet's name was Balaam. In the story, it appears that Balaam may have been rather uncertain as to the proper procedure, but he followed the leading of God and when he opened his mouth, a blessing, instead of a curse, came forth. He began by acknowledging that the words came from Jehovah, and were not of his own making.

> *"The oracle of one who sees clearly, the oracle of one who hears the words of God, who has knowledge from the Most High, who sees a vision from the Almighty, who falls prostrate, and whose eyes are opened: I see him, but not now; I behold him, but not near. A Star will come out of Jacob; a Sceptre will rise out of Israel.... A ruler will come out of Jacob."* (Numbers 24:15-19)

Balaam identified the time of the fulfilling of this prophecy. He said it was in *"the latter days."* When he said *"I see him, but not now; I behold him, but not near,"* he recognized that the fulfilling of the prophecy would be a long time in the future from his day.

Many have wondered who this prophetic Star out of Jacob, and Sceptre out of Israel is. Some have suggested that the star may have reference to the star that guided the Magi on their trip to find the baby Jesus, and that the Sceptre has reference to his right to rule at his second coming, thus placing the fulfillment of the two concepts 2,000 years apart. Yet, Balaam said that the prophecy would be for the *"latter days."*

It seems reasonable that the *"latter days,"* as mentioned here, would be the same as *"latter days,"* or *"last days,"* as is frequently mentioned throughout the Bible, having reference to the time of his second coming and the putting down of Satan's kingdom and the setting up of his glorious long-promised Kingdom of righteousness.

A similar prophetic message was given in Psalm 45:6, and its context places it at the time of the marriage of Christ and his bride. *"Your throne, O God, is forever and ever; the sceptre of your kingdom is a sceptre of righteousness."*

At first, this might seem confusing, because he is called *"God."* However the writer of the book of Hebrews quoted this prophecy and applied it to Jesus. He said, *"But unto the Son he saith, 'Thy throne, O God, is forever and ever: a sceptre of righteousness is the sceptre of thy kingdom.'"* (Hebrews 1:8) Here it clearly identifies *this "God"* as being the Son.

Balaam placed his prophecy at a time of the conquering

of Israel's enemies. The event of the conquering of her enemies in the *"latter days"* is described in Revelation 19 immediately following the marriage of the *"Bride and the Lamb."*

The *"Star out of Jacob,"* and the *"Sceptre out of Israel,"* are clearly identified by their gematria. The Star bears the number 48, both by addition and by multiplication.

$$\beth \quad \supset \quad 1 \quad \supset = \text{Star}$$

$$\beth \quad \supset \quad 1 \quad \supset$$
$$2 + 20 + 6 + 20 = 48$$

$$\beth \quad \supset \quad 1 \quad \supset$$
$$2 \times 20 \times 6 \times 20 = 4800$$

When Jesus was with his disciples on the Mount of Olives, just shortly before his death, they asked him when would be the time of his return. He gave them many signs and events that would happen, then he said *"So will be the coming of the Son of Man."* It is no mistake that the gematria for *"the coming of the Son of Man"* is 4800. That number was important in identifying him as the Star out of Jacob and the Sceptre out of Israel.

4800 = The coming of the Son of Man, η παρουσια του υιου του ανθρωπου, (Matthew 24:27)

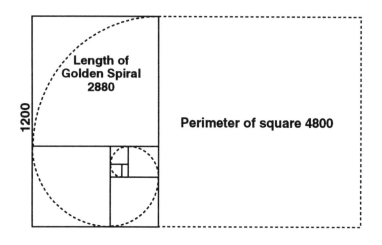

4800 = Star

4800 = The coming of the Son of Man (Matthew 24:27)

480 = The Breaker has come up, עלה הפרץ, (Prophetic of Jesus at his return, Micah 2:13)

48   = Jubilee, יובל, (Prophetic of time of Jesus' return)

2880 = The Kingdom of heaven, βασιλεια των ουρανων, (Matthew 13:47)

2880 = The joy of the Lord, την χαραν του Κυριου, (Matthew 25:21)

2880 = The Bride, the Lamb's wife, την νυμφην την γυναικα αρνιου, (Revelation 21:9)

288 = He shall be a Priest on his throne, כהן על כסאו והיה, (Zechariah 6:13)

288 = The tabernacle that shall not be taken down, אהל בל יצען, (Prophetic of the New Jerusalem, Isaiah 33:20)

1200 = I have put my spirit upon Him, נתתי רוחי עליו, (Prophetic of Jesus at his second coming, Isa. 42:1)

1200 = My righteousness shall be forever, לעולם תהיה צדקתי, (Prophetic of Jesus, Isaiah 51:8)

120 = The King, למלך, (Prophetic of Jesus when he reigns on David's throne, Zechariah 14:17)

The use of the number 12 in this Golden Rectangle is basic to the gematria of the scriptures, for the number 12 is a "foundation" number. Its multiples are part of the pattern of sacred numbers. But the number 12 is special for another very unique reason: it is the link that combines the function of ϕ (phi, .618) with the function of π (pi, 3.14159). It connects the Golden Proportion with the circle.

$$12 \div \phi \div \phi = (\pi 10)$$

or

$$12 \div .618034 \div .618034 = 31.416$$

Using this basic foundation number as the diameter of a circle, its circumference would be 37.7. This is exciting because 377 defines the Sceptre out of Israel. The statement in Hebrews 1:8 says, *"...a sceptre of righteousness is the sceptre of thy Kingdom."* The Greek word used here for *"sceptre,"* ($\rho\alpha\beta\delta o\varsigma$), is the equivalent of the Hebrew word for *"sceptre,"* (שבט), in the prophecy of Balaam.

377 = Sceptre, $\rho\alpha\beta\delta o\varsigma$

However, if we were to multiply the letter-numbers in the word *"sceptre,"* the product would be 54. The use of the number 54 in relation to the Kingdom of God is apparent in the gematria of the scriptures. It describes the return of Jesus as King on David's throne in the Kingdom of God–the time when he holds the *sceptre.*

The following are by addition:

5040 = The Kingdom of our Lord and his Christ $\beta\alpha\sigma\iota\lambda\epsilon\iota\alpha$
        $K\upsilon\rho\iota\upsilon\upsilon$ $\eta\mu\omega\nu$ $\kappa\alpha\iota$ $X\rho\iota\sigma\tau\upsilon\upsilon$ $\alpha\upsilon\tau\upsilon\upsilon$, (Rev. 11:15)

504 = The house of David, סכת דויד, (Amos 9:11)

The following are by multiplication:

5040 = Until Shiloh comes, עד כי יבא שילה, (Shiloh is his
        name at his second coming, Gen. 49:10)

504 = Christ, $X\rho\iota\sigma\tau\sigma\varsigma$

5040 = Seventh day, יום השביעי

The term *"seventh day"* is not out of place in this relationship. In Exodus 20 where the Ten Commandments were given, it states: *"For in six days Jehovah made the heavens and the earth, the sea, and all which is in them, and He rested on the seventh day."* The seventh day is divided into seven periods of 1,000 years each, six of which are the history of man from the creation of Adam until the present time, and the seventh thousand years is Earth's Great Millennium, which is considered in the scriptures as a Sabbath. It is at the beginning of that great Sabbath, or seventh day, that Jesus will return as Shiloh. Therefore the relationship of the number 5040 becomes apparent: it is pointing to the beginning of Earth's Great Millennium, the time of Jesus' return–the time when he will reign on David's throne.

It is worthy of note that the *"six days"* that are spoken of in this text are the Hebrew words ששת ימים, which multiply to 5760. It is remarkable that the Hebrew year 5760, according to the present Hebrew calendar, begins on September 11, 1999, the day of their New Year, *Rosh Hashanah.* That date will be 3,000 years from the time when David set up his kingdom in Jerusalem, and 2,000 years from the birth of Jesus. It will also be 2,966 years from the end of David's reign, the time of his death. These numbers are remarkable when related to the Golden Proportion.

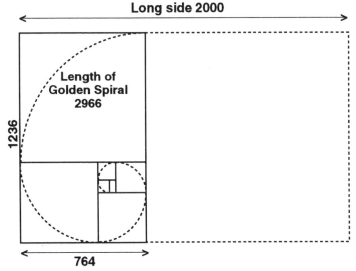

Long side 2000

Length of Golden Spiral 2966

1236

764

2,000 years from Jesus' birth to the Hebrew year 5760

2,966 years from the end of David's reign to the Hebrew year 5760

1236 = God with us (Immanuel), (Matthew 1:23)

1236 = A Root out of dry ground, שרש מארץ ציה, (Jesus is The Branch out of the root of David, Isaiah 53:2)

1236 = Chief Shepherd, $\alpha\rho\chi\iota\pi o\iota\mu\varepsilon\nu o\varsigma$, (A title given to Jesus at the time of his return, I Peter 5:4)

764 = A Shoot proceeds from the stump of Jesse, ויצא חטר מגזע ישי, (Prophetic of Jesus as The Branch out of the root of David, the son of Jesse. Isaiah 11:1)

If we placed the 2,000 years as the long side of the Golden Rectangle, and 1236 as the short side, the Golden Spiral that can be traced within it has a length of 4800.

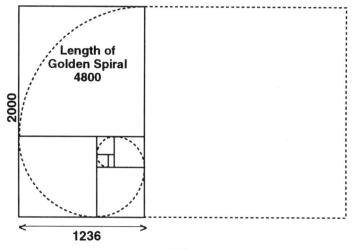

Or we could place the 2,966 years from the death of David to the Hebrew year 5760 as the short side of the Golden Rectangle, and the long side would become 4800. Thus the connection between the reign of King David and the beginning of the reign of the antitypical King David, Jesus Christ, keeps turning up the number 4800.

4800 = The coming of the Son of Man (the words of Jesus
          in Matthew 24:27)
4800 = Star (the Star out of Jacob)
480 = The Breaker has come up (King Jesus is here called
          The Breaker, Micah 2:13)
48   = Jubilee (prophetic of the time of Jesus' return)

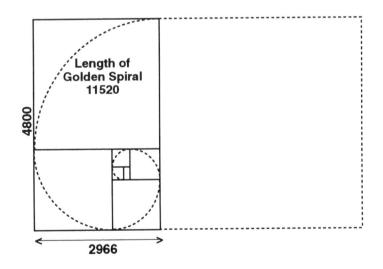

1152 = Kingdom of God (Matthew 21:31)
1152 = The throne of David (Isa. 9:6, by multiplication)

There appears to be a prophetic and chronological link between the time of David's reign and the second coming of Jesus, relating to the Hebrew year 5760. More will be said on this in a later chapter. But for now, let's find out who The Breaker is, and why this title was given to him by the prophet.

> *"I will surely gather all of you, Jacob; I will surely gather the remnant of Israel.... The Breaker has come up before them; they have broken up and have passed through the gate and have gone out by it. And their King shall pass through before them, and Jehovah at the head of them."* (Micah 2:13)

Joseph Seiss, in his wonderful book, *Gospel in the Stars* identifies this statement of Micah with the constellation called The Breaker, or Perseus, which is one of the decans of the Zodiacal sign of Aries, the Ram. As Seiss set forth the beautiful story of the whole plan of salvation as pictured in the progression of the sun through the Zodiac, the constellation of Aries and its decans foretell the time when Jesus takes his great power and reigns. The constellation of The Breaker depicts a conquering warrior, named Perseus, representing the returned Lord taking his power primarily over Satan, whose severed head he holds under his left arm.

His identification as The Breaker fits the time and event

of the breaking of the seven seals of Revelation 5. He is the one found worthy to break the seals, thus he is The Breaker.

Joseph Seiss describes him thus:

> Micah prophesies of a time when the flock of God shall be gathered, their King pass before them, and the Lord on the head of them; and says that this shall be when "The Breaker is come up before them." ...The Breaker must needs be Christ...breaking the way of His people. So the Lamb of the Apocalypse is The Breaker of the seals and of the apostate nations, the same as the Son in the second Psalm. And this Breaker, in these very acts, is the precise picture in this constellation.[1]

Although Seiss' identification of The Breaker is apparently accurate, yet we need leave nothing to conjecture, for the gematria of his name makes the positive identification. The name Breaker, in Hebrew, is פרץ, and it adds to 370. The number 37 is a prime, and it is a very special number in the gematria of the scriptures, for it is the basis of most of the names and titles of Jesus and his work with the Father in the creation of all things. (Please see Appendix II.)

---

1   Joseph A. Seiss, *Gospel in the Stars*, Kregel Publications, Grand Rapids, Michigan, 1972, p. 96

Micah places this name, The Breaker, into a statement of action. He says, *"The Breaker has come up."* The addition of the letter-numbers becomes 480. Yes, it is that special number that appears to be associated with the link between the reigns of David and Jesus, the typical and the antitypical King. Could this identifying number have been encoded into the prophecy to denote the time of his return?

This prophecy of Micah appears to be telling us the same story as we found in the prophecy of Balaam, that a Star (which adds to 48 and multiplies to 4800) would come forth out of Jacob. That Star, prophetic of the returned Lord, now becomes the constellation of The Breaker, also picturing the returned Lord, the King who will sit on David's throne. *"The coming of the Son of Man,"* adds to 4800.

Could the 2,000 years from Jesus' birth to the Hebrew year 5760 be related to the gematria of his promise: *"and my reward is with me,"* και ο μισθος μου μετ εμου?

2000 = And my reward is with me (Revelation 22:12)

While we are talking about the Star, let's digress just a bit and include a few more stars. There is another constellation that bears exciting relationships to The Number of His Name. It is the well-known constellation that is probably the first one that we notice when we look into the night sky. It is Ursa Major, commonly called the Big

Dipper. For centuries, men have used this obvious constellation to point the way to North. Its two bright stars, Dubhe and Merak, point directly to the pole star.

This big bear has a companion, the little bear, known as Ursa Minor. The last star in its upturned tail *is* the pole star.

Joseph Seiss shows the relationship of these two bears with the ingathering of all into Christ's kingdom. The little bear representing the ingathering of the saints, to be with him in his position of ruler in the North. The big bear representing the ingathering of Israel and all the remainder of mankind who desire to come into the blessings of that kingdom. The big bear represents those who are spoken of in Revelation 22: 17, *"Whoever is thirsty, let him take the free gift of the water of life."*

Jesus said something very similar to this when he was here on earth. It was at the time of the celebration of the Feast of Tabernacles. At the end of the seven days of the festival, they celebrated the Great Eighth Day of the Feast. On that day, which pictures God's Great 8th Day, Jesus stood up and said *"If any man is thirsty, let him come unto me and drink."*

The Feast of Tabernacles was called the Feast of Ingathering, for it followed the final harvest of their crops. It pictured the great ingathering of all into Christ's kingdom during Earth's Great Millennium, followed by the Great 8th Day.

With this beautiful picture in mind, let's look at the

geometry of that constellation. We call it the Big Dipper. The cup of that dipper is the bottom portion of a pentagon.

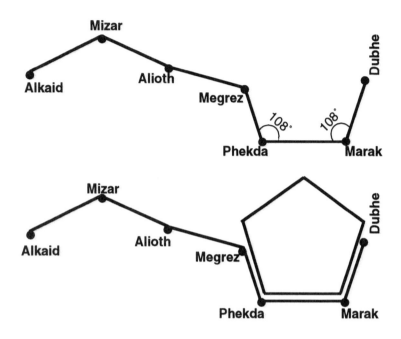

Again the 1 and the 8 makes its appearance–the numbers of beginning and new beginning. The number 108 is the gematria for *"red,"* pointing to the shed blood of Jesus. For it was only through Jesus that this ingathering of all mankind can become a reality. And when we multiply the 108, that is so prominent in the constellation, by the number 48, which, as we have seen, is the gematria for the Star out of Jacob, the product is 5,184. Since there are five such angles of 108°, let's multiply this by five, (5,184 x 5 = 25,920) and the product is the number of years of the grand celestial cycle of the sun through all twelve signs of the Zodiac. This is exciting! It is telling us that this constellation, which we see beautifully displayed every night in the northern sky, is a dramatic sign of the completion of the work of redemption and restoration through Jesus Christ. The number 25,920 is the number of years in the Great Year. It both adds and multiplies to 18.

$$2 + 5 + 9 + 2 = 18$$
$$2 \times 5 \times 9 \times 2 = 180$$

25,920 ÷ 3168 (Lord Jesus Christ) = 8.181818 to infinity.

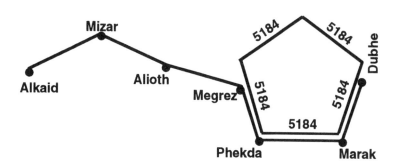

The following are by multiplication:

5184 = The Lord hath prepared his throne in the heavens, יהוה בשמים הכין כסאו, (Psalm 103:19)

5184 = The ransomed of the Lord shall return, פדויי יהוה ישבון, (Isaiah 35:10)

5184 = The heavens and the earth, השמים ואת הארץ, (Exodus 20:11)

5184 = My holy Jerusalem, קדשי ירושלם

JESUS CHRIST: THE NUMBER OF HIS NAME

The prophecy of Balaam was of a *Star out of Jacob*, and a *Sceptre out of Israel*. We have seen how the Star, 48, is shown in the pentagon whose sides are 5184. The relationship of the Sceptre is also apparent, and it shows us the interaction of the pentagon with the Golden Proportion. A square with a perimeter of 518.4 will project a Golden Rectangle whose long side is 129.6 and whose Golden Spiral is 311. Sceptre, שבט, adds to 311.

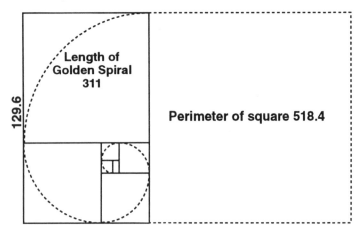

311 = Sceptre, שבט

1296 = (12 x 108) My salvation from generation to generation, ישועתי לדור דורים, (Isaiah 51:8)

1296 = Prince of Peace, שר שלום, (Isaiah 9:6 by multiplication)

5184 = Behold, I am sending my Messenger and he shall prepare the way before me. And the Lord, whom you seek, shall suddenly come to his temple, even

> the Messenger of the Covenant, in whom you
> delight. Behold he comes. (Malachi 3:1)

The *Messenger of the Covenant* is the Lord Jesus Christ at his return. This title, when written in Greek, has a number value of 1080. The numbers are so expertly interwoven that I can only stand in amazement! The foundation number, 12, when multiplied by 108 produces 1296, the long side of the above Golden Rectangle. It is suggested that when Jesus returns, he will be the Messenger of the Covenant, the Star out of Jacob, and the Sceptre of Israel.

The pentagon, that fits precisely into the cup of the Big Dipper not only tells of His return but also of the work of redemption and reconciliation, by its amazing number relationships. With this in mind, let's look more closely at the pentagon. It has a wonderful story to tell.

To construct a pentagon we start with a square, then project its Golden Rectangle. Note the close relationship between the pentagon and the Golden Proportion. We'll begin by drawing a square with sides of 1 unit.

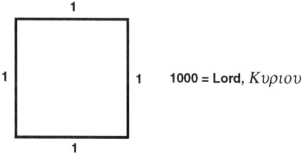

1000 = Lord, *Κυριου*

Next, we extend one side of the square to project its Golden Rectangle. Its proportions now become the Golden Proportion, 1:1.618.

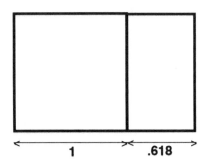

Using the Golden Rectangle as the foundation, with compass and straightedge, a pentagon can be drawn that will have sides of 1 unit.

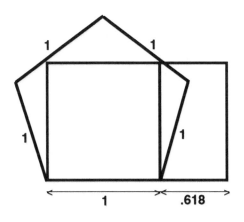

Let's suppose that the 1 unit is 1 mile. I've chosen the mile unit because of its amazing relationship to the gematria of the Bible. One mile contains 5,280 feet. And it has been observed that 528 is the gematria for the first work of creation, the *"breaking forth of light";* it is also the gematria for *"the dawn"* (both are translated from the same Hebrew word, כשחר); it is also the gematria for *"the Key"* of the house of David. Jesus, at his return, holds this key and unlocks the house of David and becomes the king on David's throne. He becomes King at *"the dawn"* of Earth's Great Millennium. This number, 528, is also used to identify the time of his second coming, which will usher in the thousand years of the ingathering of mankind into sonship with God–the sonship that Adam lost through disobedience.

The third chapter of the book of Malachi not only identifies the Messenger of the Covenant at the time of his return, and the numbers 108 and 5184, which are used so beautifully in the pentagon, but this prophecy also identifies the return of Jesus. Malachi asks the question, *"Who can endure the day of His coming?"* The gematria of the time is the beautiful 528.

---

528 = The Day of His coming

ומי את יום בואו

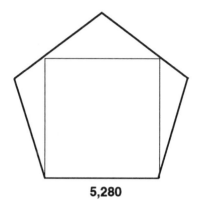

5,280

If one side now equals 1 mile (5,280 feet), the perimeter of the pentagon will be 316,800 inches. It bears the number of the Lord Jesus Christ, *Κυριος Ιησους Χριστος*, 3168. Stated in yards it will be 79,200, which represents the whole earth–the world-wide work of redemption and reconciliation–for the diameter of the earth is 7,920 miles, and the number 792 is the gematria for *"salvation,"* ישועות.

Using the mile unit, the perimeter of the square becomes 21,120 feet. This number beautifully tells of the sending of the only-begotten son of God to earth to be man's Redeemer, for 2112 is the gematria for *"A virgin shall conceive and bear a son and shall call his name Emmanuel,"* (Isaiah 7:14)

The next time the night is clear, and the stars are bright, look up at Ursa Major who seemingly dominates the northern sky and know that it is a "sign," it is an assurance that the redeeming work of Christ is progressing grandly on to its fulfillment.

The height of the fantastic pentagon that can be inscribed within the cup of this constellation, based on the mile unit, will be 1.53884 miles. If we drew a square on this height, (1.53884^2) it would be filled with 2,368 square miles. The gematria for Jesus Christ, *Ιησους Χριστος*, is 2368. The numbers and their relationships are nothing of man's invention. They are the signature of the Creator!

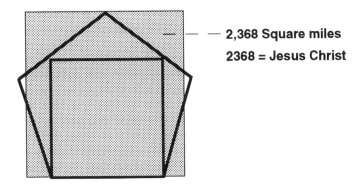

— — 2,368 Square miles
2368 = Jesus Christ

When we connect the points of the pentagon, we are drawing a perfect five-pointed star–the pentagram. Note its obvious relation to the Golden Proportion. It is replete with them.

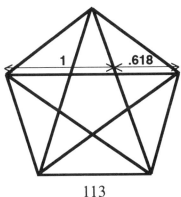

Because of the relationship of the pentagram to the Golden Proportion (ϕ), the Pythagoreans wore it as a symbol of their society. Pythagoras, however, did not invent, nor discover it. The pentagram was used by the Babylonians and the Egyptians long before Pythagoras. But its beautiful display of the Golden Proportion tells us that it is part of the fabric of creation.

The inter-relationship of the Golden Proportion with the pentagon is also apparent from the gematria of the scriptures. The grand celestial cycle of the heavens, the progression of the sun through the twelve signs of the Zodiac, called the Great Year, connects with the Golden Proportion in a remarkably wonderful way. The length of the Great Year is 25,920 years.

2592 = The heart of Jerusalem,
לב ירושלם, (Isaiah 40:2
by multiplication)

618 = The heart of Jerusalem,
(Isaiah 40:2 by addition)

"Comfort, comfort my people, says your God. Speak to the heart of Jerusalem, and call to her, that her warfare is done, that her iniquity is pardoned..." (Isaiah 40:1-2)

8
Jesus Christ
and the Grand Octave

The concept of the Grand Octave of time has come down to us from many of the ancient writers. It is the idea that seven periods of time are followed by an eighth, which begins the cycle all over again. But this octave is a compound one, in which the seventh period is successively divided into seven more; however, each seventh period is followed by the same eighth period. It's not as complicated as it sounds.

A manuscript known as *The Secrets of Enoch,* of unknown origin, but translated into the Greek language around the beginning of the Christian era, is quite clear as to the author's concept of the octave of time. This document was known to the early church fathers, and its influence can be seen in their work. It has, in modern times, been translated into English. Chapter 33 begins with this revealing statement, written as if God were doing the speaking:

> And I blessed the seventh day, which is the Sabbath, on which I rested from all my works. And I appointed the eighth day also, that the eighth day should be the first-created after my work, and that the first seven revolve in the form of

the seventh thousand, and that at the beginning
of the eighth thousand there should be a time
of not-counting, endless.... I am self-eternal,
not made with hands, and without change.

By definition, he is saying that 7,000 years became the
7th of the creative six, thus making the 8th day not only
the 8th for man's experience, but also the 8th on God's
great work week. This is in harmony with the number symbology in the Bible, in which the number 1 represents
Beginning and the number 8 represents a New Beginning,
and, by extension, 1 represents the Beginner, and 8 represents the New Beginner. This New Beginning for man was
made possible through Jesus, and the letter-numbers of
his name, in Greek, add to 888.

When he is King during the 7th thousand-year span, it
is said of him, *"He must reign until he has put all enemies
under his feet."* The letter-numbers of that glorious promise add to 8888. The end of that phase of his reign, following the putting of all enemies under his feet, will be the
beginning of the Great Eighth Day – the New Beginning.

Another book, written by the Apostle Paul's companion, Barnabas, sometime during the first century A.D. gives
the same analogy of the octave of time. He wrote:

Even in the beginning of Creation he makes
mention of the Sabbath. And God made in six
days the works of his hands; and he rested the
seventh day, and sanctified it. Consider, my

> children, what that signifies–he finished them in six days. The meaning of it is this: that in six thousand years shall all things be accomplished. Then he shall gloriously rest in that seventh day.... When resting from all things I shall begin the eighth day, that is, the beginning of the other world.

Barnabas was describing the 6,000 years followed by a 7th, just as there were 6 divisions of creation, followed by a 7th. All of which are followed by the Great Eighth Day – the New Beginning.

In the Babylonian Talmud (A.D. 200-400) there is a large section in which several prominent Rabbis express their opinion on the time of the coming of the Messiah. Rabbi Kattina wrote:

> The world endures 6,000 years, and one thousand it shall be laid waste, that is, the enemies of God shall be laid waste, whereof it is said, "The Lord alone shall be exalted in that day." As out of seven years every seventh is a year of remission, so out of the seven thousand years of the world, the seventh millennium shall be the 1,000 years of remission, that God alone may be exalted in that day.

Another reference in the Talmud to the same Rabbi is as follows:

> It has been taught in accordance with Rabbi

God's Grand Work Week, and The Octave

1	2	3	4	5	6	7	Creation's Grand Octave
Light	Waters Divided	Dry Land and Vegetation	Sun & Moon shine on the Earth	Fish & Birds	Mammals & Man	God Rested	

3,000 years from Adam to King David			3,000 years from King David to King Messiah			Millennium	God's Great 8th Day
1,000 years	1,000 years	1,000 years	1,000 years	1,000 years	1,000 years	1,000 years	

Earth's Great Millennium pictured by the 7 days of the Feast of Tabernacles							Pictured by Great 8th day of the Feast
day 1	day 2	day 3	day 4	day 5	day 6	day 7	

> Kattina: just as the seventh year is one year of
> release in seven, so is the world: one thousand
> years out of seven shall be fallow, as it is writ-
> ten and the Lord shall alone be exalted in that
> day.

Another ancient manuscript, the book of II Esdras, was written sometime during the first century before Christ, with its first and last chapters having been added by a later writer sometime during the first century of the Christian era. In it, Esdras (a pseudo name) was describing an encounter he had with the angel Uriel, who told him that there had been 3,000 years from Adam to King David. We do not know for sure if Uriel actually told the writer this, or if this pseudo Esdras (the Greek name for Ezra), was simply writing a good story. Either way, it still reflects the knowledge available to the writer at that time.

It appears to have been the belief that man's current experience covers a span of 6,000 years, followed by a Sabbath–all of which is a Sabbath on God's great work week, to be followed by the New Beginning. Thus it has come down to us from ancient times and is still believed by many today.

This Grand Octave of time is similar in concept to the musical octave. The seven tone scale has been handed down to us from time immemorial, however, in ancient times it was thought of as descending, rather than ascending. The notes were played "down" the scale, as if descending from heaven. Because of this, the names for the tones were devised to portray this divine origin. We know these notes, in descending order, as DO–SI–LA–SOL–FA–MI–RE–DO. They were given these names by Guido d'Arezzo around A.D. 1000. These popular names are really only the first letters of their Latin names, whose meaning reveals their cosmological structure.

DOminus	"Lord"	Absolute (the Beginner)
SIder	"Stars"	All Galaxies
LActea	"Milk"	Earth's Galaxy, the Milky Way
SOL	"Sun"	Sun
FAta	"Fate"	The Planets
MIcrocosmos	"Small Universe"	The Earth
REgina Coeli	"Queen of the Heavens"	Moon
DOminus	"Lord"	Absolute (the New Beginner)

It becomes apparent that the scale was meant to model the macrocosmic design–the universe ruled by the octave. It originates from above, and starts with the Absolute, the Creator, the Beginner, and descends through a seven stage hierarchy, and returns again to the Absolute. This time it is the New Beginner, but the same musical tone. It begins the next series of seven. The 1 and the 8 become the same.

Tighten a string between two points and pluck it. Then hold it down in the middle and pluck each half–it will be the same note as the whole string, but higher. Harmony is born when the full string is divided into unequal parts at a place where both parts produce the same note, an octave apart.

Pythagoras discovered that the balancing point came at two-thirds of the string. When the string is held down at this point, both sides will sound the same, an octave apart.

Pluck the full string, then two-thirds of the string. Regardless of the original tone, its two-thirds tone has something special that we can feel, and enter into as we listen to it. It is traditionally known as the "chord of triumph" because of its special reaction on the human psyche. The sound produced by the two-thirds position is the fifth tone from the whole string. If the whole string produced the note "C," the fifth tone would be "G." When played together, they produce the "chord of triumph."

The 7,000 years of man's experience, leading to and culminating in the Great Eighth Day can be likened to the string stretched between two points. Pluck the string and the tone we hear represents the Beginning and the New Beginning–both ends of the octave. Pluck it at two-thirds and we have the time when salvation was made possible by the death of Jesus. Pluck the two together and we have the "chord of triumph" – the great resounding harmony of God's work of salvation, restitution and reconciliation completed.

Each note of the musical scale is a set of vibrations. Our brain translates those vibrations into sounds. It is thrilling to realize that the vibrations per second in the notes that produce this "chord of triumph," are the identical numbers that describe and define the work of creation, salvation, and reconciliation. It is too astounding to be mere coincidence.

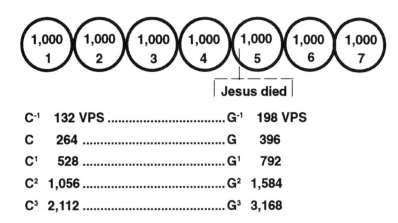

	Jesus died	
C^{-1} 132 VPS	G^{-1}	198 VPS
C 264	G	396
C^1 528	G^1	792
C^2 1,056	G^2	1,584
C^3 2,112	G^3	3,168

The number of vibrations per second in the "C" column are numbers that relate to the Beginning and the New Beginning (Beginner and New Beginner), the 1 and the 8–the octave.

1320 = He made him (man) in the likeness of God
בדמות אלהים עשה אתו, (Genesis 5:1)

1302 = The Creator, $\tau o \nu$ $\kappa \tau \iota \sigma \alpha \nu \tau \alpha$, (Rom. 2:47)

132 = The Lord your God, יהוה אלהיכם, (Joshua 4:5)

132 = God divided, אלהים יבדל, (creation is growth by division, Genesis 1)

132 = Make whole, $\iota \alpha o \mu \alpha \iota$, (man's restored condition)

2640 = His throne, τον θρονον αυτον, (Rev. 1:5)

264 = Truth, αληθειας, (Jesus was the personification of truth.)

264 = Generation (beginning), γενεας, (Luke 11:50)

528 = The breaking forth of light, כשחר (the first act of creation)

528 = The Key, מפתח

5028 = The Lamb slain from the foundation of the world, του αρνιου του εσφαγμενου απο καταβολης κοσμου, (Rev. 13:8)

1056 = I form the light, I create darkness, אור ובורא חשך יוצר, (Isaiah 45:7)

1056 = His dominion is an everlasting dominion that will not pass away, שלטנה שלטן עלם די לא יעדה, (Dan. 7:14)

1056 = The joy of thy salvation, ששון ישעך, (51:12)

2112 = Glory of the Lord, δοξης του κυριου, (II Thess. 2:14)

2112 = A virgin shall conceive and bear a son and shall call his name Emmanuel, בן וקראת שמו עמנו אל העלמה הרה וילדת, (Isaiah 7:14)

All of the vibrations per second in the "G" column are numbers that relate to the means of salvation, Jesus Christ, and the only place (so far as we are aware) in the Universe where salvation has been given–the earth. Note that the numbers that represent salvation are also the numbers in the geometry of the earth–it identifies the *place* of salvation.

1,980 miles, one quarter of earth's diameter

198 = He is altogether lovely, כלו מחמדים, (Prophetic of Jesus, Song of Solomon 5:16)

198 = The king in his beauty, מלך ביפיו, (Isa. 33:17)

3,960 miles, radius of earth

396 = Salvation, הישועה, (Isaiah 12:3)

396 = Purification, מרוקים

396 = On the earth, על הארץ, (Genesis 1:15)

7,920 miles, diameter of earth

792 = Salvation, ישועות, (Psalm 116:13)

792 = He shall see the travail of His soul, עמל נפשו יראה, (Prophetic of Jesus on the cross, Isaiah 53:11)

1,584 miles, one fifth of earth's diameter

1584= Beautiful for situation, the joy of the whole earth, is Mount Zion, יפה נוף משוש כל הארץ הר ציון, (Psalm 48:2)

1584 = I have established my covenant, והקמתי את בריתי, (God's covenant with man, never to destroy the earth, Genesis 9:11)

31,680 miles, perimeter of square around earth (or 4 times
   the earth's diameter)

3168 = Lord Jesus Christ, *Κυριος Ιησους Χριστος*

3168 = The Son of Man, *η υιου του ανθρωπου*

3168 = Mediator between God and man, *μεσιτης Θεου
   και ανθρωπων,* (Jesus, I Timothy 2:5)

It becomes obvious that music is dominated by the number 7, however, we always think of it as 8, and call it an octave. The eighth note, however, is actually the first note in the next series of seven. Thus 1 and 8 become inseparable as the numbers of Beginning and New Beginning.

This relationship is made even more apparent in a seven-sided figure, a heptagon. In a heptagon with a side measure of 1 unit, its heptagram will have lengths of 1.8 units between all of its points.

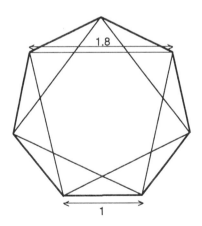

The seventh note in this Grand Octave of time, can again be divided into seven periods. It is the prophetic fulfillment of the Feast of Tabernacles.

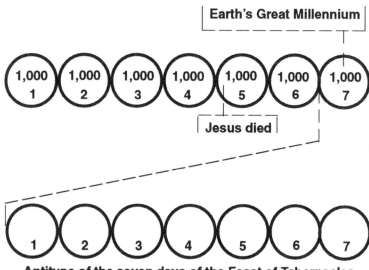

Antitype of the seven days of the Feast of Tabernacles
Earth's Great Millennium

God instructed Moses to have the Israelites celebrate three special feasts during each year. These are recorded in Exodus 23:

> *"Three times a year you are to celebrate a festival to me. Celebrate the Feast of Unleavened Bread.... Celebrate the Feast of Harvest.... Celebrate the Feast of Ingathering at the end of the year.... Three*

*times a year all the men are to appear
before the Sovereign Lord."*

These three festivals are better known to us as Passover, Pentecost, and Tabernacles. The Feast of Unleavened bread included the Passover, which really began the night before with the killing of the Passover lamb. It also included the offering of the firstfruits of the barley harvest, known to us as the Wave-Sheaf Offering, or the Omer. Fifty days after this Wave-Sheaf Offering, was the Feast of Pentecost, which was the offering of the firstfruits of the wheat harvest. Then there was a long gap until the autumn, when they celebrated the final feast of the year, the Feast of Tabernacles. It was the ingathering of the final fruit of the harvest. This celebration lasted seven days, followed by a special day of feasting and happiness–a day of rest, in which no servile work was to be done.

There were 186 days between the killing of the Passover lamb and the end of the 7th day of Tabernacles, using inclusive counting, which is always used when counting Hebrew time.

Israel celebrated other feasts, but these three were the ones during which all the males were to present themselves to the Lord at their sacred center. After David's kingdom was set up in Jerusalem, that became the place to which all the males would travel for these special days. Thus, they became known as the "pilgrim festivals."

Simply stated, these three festivals were an illustration

of salvation through Jesus Christ. The killing of the Passover lamb was obviously an illustration of the death of the Lamb of God, Jesus Christ. And to emphasize this fact, Jesus died on the very day and at the very hour in which Israel was killing their Passover lambs. Even the gematria of the two are the same.

1480 = Christ, $X\rho\iota\sigma\tau\circ\varsigma$

148   = Passover, פסח

The Apostle Paul left nothing to our conjecture; he clearly stated that *"Christ, our Passover, is sacrificed for us,"* (I Cor. 5:7).

The second pilgrim festival, Pentecost, was an illustration of the age in which the church is called and developed, and finally presented to God. It began on the day of Pentecost following the death of Jesus, with the anointing of the Holy Spirit upon that small beginning, and continues until the return of Jesus to claim his bride and present her to God. On the day of Pentecost, the Israelites were to present two loaves, baked with flour from the new wheat harvest. It represented the presenting of his church to the Father.

And the final pilgrim festival, in which all males were to present themselves before God, was the Feast of Tabernacles. This was also called the Feast of Ingathering, because it came at the close of the final harvest of their crops. It was a joyous occasion, and lasted seven days. In

Jewish liturgy it came to be known as "The season of our joy." This celebration is an illustration of Earth's Great Millennium, at the close of which, man will be fully reconciled to God.

It was called the Feast of Tabernacles because during that week the people were to build booths, or tabernacles, from boughs and branches, and live in them. It was sort of like camping out.

Nehemiah instructed the people, *"Go, eat the fat, and drink the sweet, and send portions to him for whom nothing is prepared,"* (Neh. 8:10). It was a time of good things to eat, and of sharing with others; and also a time of the reading of the Law. *"Day by day, from the first day until the last day, he* (Ezra) *read the book of the Law of God. And they kept the feast seven days,"* (Neh. 8:18).

This same illustration of eating the fat and drinking the sweet drinks was used prophetically of the time of Earth's Great Millennium, in the prophecy of Isaiah.

> *"And Jehovah of hosts shall make for all people a feast of fat things in this mountain; a feast of wine on the lees, of fat things full of marrow, of wine on the lees well refined. And He will destroy in this mountain the face of the covering which covers all people, and the veil that is woven over all nations. He will swallow up death in victory! And the Lord Jehovah will wipe*

129

away tears from all faces. And he shall remove the reproach of his people from all the earth–for Jehovah has spoken. And one shall say in that day, 'This is our God, we have waited for him, he will save us; this is Jehovah, we have waited for him; we will be glad and rejoice in his salvation,'" (Isaiah 25:7-9)

The prophet Zechariah described this same time, and said that all people would then celebrate the Feast of Tabernacles. He was talking about Earth's Great Millennium.

"And the Lord shall be King over all the earth; in that day there shall be one God and his name one.... And it shall be that everyone...shall go up from year to year to worship the King, the Lord of Hosts, and to keep the Feast of Tabernacles," (Zech. 14)

A part of the ceremonial service of this feast was called "Joy of the house of drawing." It was the drawing of water. Every morning of the feast, while the morning sacrifice was being prepared, a joyous procession, accompanied by music, and headed by a priest carrying a golden pitcher, made its way from the Temple to the Pool of Siloam. There they drew water from the pool, and returned to the Temple. With excitement and joy, the water was poured into a silver basin on the altar.

This joyous ritual of the drawing of water is the background for another prophecy of Isaiah regarding the time of Earth's Great Millennium.

> *"And you shall with joy draw water out of the wells of salvation. And in that day you shall say, 'Praise Jehovah! Call on His name; declare His doings among the people; make mention that His name is exalted.'"* (Isaiah 12:3)

The gematria of this text is also descriptive of the day of salvation–the day when the people will draw the water of life from the wells of salvation. The word *"wells"* in this text is the Hebrew word *"ma'yan,"* מעיני, which is translated in other places *"fountains,"* or *"springs."* It describes a continual and abundant source of fresh, pure water. The addition of its letter-numbers is 180. Again the 1 and the 8 become apparent as the source of life.

The Hebrew word used here for Salvation adds to 396, which, as has been shown, relates to the earth as the place of salvation, 3,960 miles being the radius of earth.

Thus *"Wells of Salvation"* has a total number value of 576 (180 + 396 = 576). It possibly has reference to the time of the beginning of the Millennium, the Hebrew year 5760.

When this number–576– is the measure of the perimeter of a square, the Golden Rectangle that can be projected on that square has a long side of 144, and the Golden Rectangle inscribed within it has a length of 345.6.

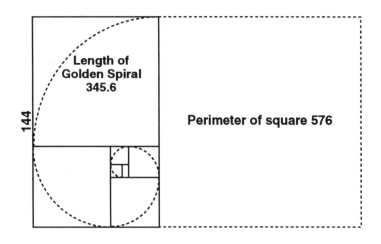

When applied to the Millennium, these numbers have remarkable significance. As previously shown, the number 576 is related to the ending of the 6 days (6,000 years), and the beginning of the 7th day, the Millennial day (1,000 years). This is shown in several places in scripture, relating the 6 days as being separated from the 7th, which is a Sabbath. The Hebrew words *"six days,"* ששת ימים, multiply to 576. It is not a coincidence that the Hebrew year 5760 begins our next millennium. That year begins with Rosh Hashanah, which, on the Roman calendar will be September 11, 1999. I do not predict what events will happen in that year; I merely call attention to it as apparently being the beginning of Earth's Great Millennium.

However, from the prophetic scriptures, I can suggest what will happen *during* that Millennium. It is a time of salvation and reconciliation, at the end of which, mankind will be fully reconciled to God. All that Adam lost, through disobedience, will be restored to man. This is the significance of the long side of the Golden Rectangle being 144. It is a number that always has reference to God's realm.

The Hebrew word that means "that which has no beginning nor ending" is מדק, and it adds to 144. The word is used often in the scriptures, sometimes translated *"beginning,"* sometimes *"everlasting,"* sometimes *"eternal."* Those who are in God's realm often bear this number. It is consistent throughout the Bible. The word *"believers,"* πιστων, adds to 1440. This number applies to those who are believers now, but it will also apply at the end of the Millennium, when man will have been fully reconciled to God–they will be *"believers."* The appearance of the number 144 in the above Golden Rectangle is revealing the truth that the Apostle Paul spoke, when he described the end of the Millennium and the work of reconciling man to God.

> *"Then cometh the end, when He shall have delivered up the Kingdom to God, even the Father; when He shall have put down all rule and all authority and power. For He must reign until He has put all enemies*

under His feet. The last enemy that shall be
destroyed is death.... And when all things
shall be subdued unto him, then shall the
Son also himself be subject unto him that
put all things under him, that God may be
all in all." (I Cor. 15:24-28)

The three numbers displayed in the above Golden Proportion, in fact, show the beginning of that Millennium,
its duration and its work, and its glorious ending. It is based
on the perimeter of the square, 576, which is the gematria
for *"Wells of Salvation."* It will be during that great
antitypical Feast of Tabernacles, that the "Joy of the House
of drawing," –the drawing of the water of life from the
Wells of Salvation–will become a happy reality. Let's look
at the gematria–it is beautiful!

576 = Wells of Salvation, מעיני הישועה

576 = Life, πνευμα

576 = In God is my salvation, על אלהים ישעי, (Psa. 62:7)

576 = Eternal redemption, αιωνιαν λυτρωσιν, (by
multiplication, Hebrews 9:12)

576 = The Way of holiness, ודרך הקדש, (by multiplication, Isaiah 35:8, speaking of the way for all mankind to come to God during the Millennium.)

576 = Messiah the Prince, משיח נגיד, (by multiplication,
Daniel 9:25, speaking of the time when Jesus reigns
on the Throne of David during the Millennium.)

576 = He shall appear in His glory, נראה בכבודו, (by multiplication, Psalm 102:16, referring to the time of Jesus' return and taking his place on the Throne of David.)

576 = His Kingdom, מלכות, (by multiplication)

The use of the number 576 in relation to the Kingdom and the Millennium is amazing. And this is only a sampling of it. In the prophecy of Zechariah, we are given a description of this promised Kingdom.

> *"His feet shall stand in that day on the Mount of Olives, which is before Jerusalem on the east.... And shall come the Lord my God and all his Saints with Him.... And it will be one day* (the Millennial day), *known to the Lord; not day, not night, but it will be at evening time there will be light* (by the end of the thousand years the earth will be fully illuminated with the power and presence and favor of God). *And it shall be in that day, living waters shall go out from Jerusalem...and the Lord shall be King over all the earth."* (Zechariah 14: 4-9)

When Zechariah described *"The Lord my God and all his Saints,"* he was using a phrase that adds to 576. How beautifully the numbers tell the story. And what a beautiful story–salvation for man and reconciliation with God, to all that Adam had before he sinned.

JESUS CHRIST: THE NUMBER OF HIS NAME

The length of the Golden Spiral inscribed within the above Golden Rectangle is 345.6. It is a number that is used throughout the gematria of the scriptures to denote the final outcome, both for those who will be the heavenly bride, and for all mankind who will enjoy the living waters that nourish and refresh them during that Kingdom of peace. Here is a sampling of the use of this number:

3456 = Alpha and Omega, the beginning and the end, *αλφα και το Ω η αρχη και το τελος,* (Rev. 1:8)

3456 = The city of my God, *της πολεως του Θεου μου,* (Revelation 3:12)

3456 = The marriage of the Lamb and his Bride, *ο γαμος του αρνιου και η γυνη αυτου,* (Revelation 19:7)

3456 = The Feast of Tabernacles, חג הסכות (by multiplication, Zechariah 14:18)

3456 = His Kingdom, מלכותו, (by multiplication, Psalm 145:13)

3456 = His dominion, ממשלתו, (by multiplication, Psalm 103:22)

3456 = His throne in the heavens, בשמים הכין כסאו , (by multiplication, Psalm 103:19)

3456 = All His work, כל מלאכתו, (by multiplication, Genesis 2:3)

The Wells of Salvation will be a spring of living water that will heal the effects of the sin that Adam brought into the world. The prophet Ezekiel (chapter 47) had a vision regarding this life-giving stream, that starts as a small rivulet, and finally becomes waters too deep and too wide to cross. This torrent finally runs into the Dead Sea, and heals its waters so that it is a live sea. It is a beautiful word picture of the water of life, flowing from the Wells of Salvation. And just as the prophecy of Zechariah described a day that would be light at evening, so too this ever increasing river of life, by the end of the Millennium, will be a torrent that floods the Dead Sea (man under the Adamic curse) and causes it to flourish with life.

That River of Life is Jesus Christ. The addition of the letter-numbers of *"River of Life,"* ποταμος ζωης, (Rev. 22:1) is 1776. He is Lord of this great Sabbath Day, the seventh in man's experience on this earth–the Millennium. The letter-numbers for *"Lord of the Sabbath,"* Κυριος σαββατου, also add to 1776.

The rock that the Israelites carried with them was their source of water during their 40-year trek through the desert. In Nehemiah 9:15 reference is made to the fact that they obtained water from that rock. *"And you gave them bread from heaven for their hunger, and brought forth water for them out of the rock, for their thirst."* The Hebrew text turns the sentence around and speaks of *"water from the rock,"* ומים מסלע, and its letter-numbers add to 296.

It was life-giving water. Without it the Israelites would have died of thirst in the desert. It is worthy of note that the gematria for *"water from the rock,"* 296, is the same as *"eternal salvation,"* σωτηριας αιωνιου, 2960. And surely the one is a symbol of the other. Even *"water pitcher,"* κεραμιον, (Mark 14:13) adds to the same number, 296.

The Apostle Paul (I Corinthians 10:4-4) left no doubt as to the meaning of the water from the rock. He said the Rock was Christ. He left no doubt, also, regarding the fact that the rock was portable–they carried it with them.

> *"All did eat the same spiritual meat* (the manna); *and all did drink the same spiritual drink: for they drank of that spiritual Rock that followed* (they carried with) *them: and that Rock was Christ."*

The Greek word used here, and translated *"followed,"* is ακολουθουσης, and it means *"to carry with,"* or *"to accompany."*

This rock, from which they obtained water, was symbolic and prophetic of Jesus Christ, the source of life for all mankind. It is in the Millennium, the great antitypical Feast of Tabernacles, when he will be a River of Life, bringing water to all from the Wells of Salvation.

Again, the Golden Proportion boldly shows this relationship, for a square whose perimeter is 296, when its Golden Proportion is projected, will produce a Golden Spiral with a length of 177.6. They are not random numbers. They tell the wonderful story of salvation and life. And the gematria for *"spiritual Rock,"* πνευματικης πετρας, is 1800, bearing the number of the Beginner and the New Beginner.

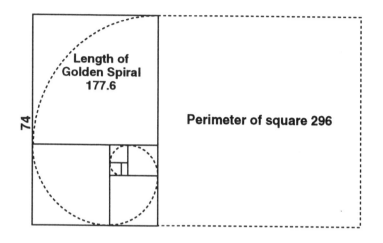

The long side of the above Golden Rectangle has a measure of 74. It is one of the foundation numbers of the sacred code of scripture. Even the word *"foundation,"* in Hebrew, עד, has the value of 74. But the Apostle Paul, in I Corinthians 3:11 said, *"Other foundation can no man lay, than that is laid, which is Jesus Christ."* The shedding of his blood as a ransom for man, is the very foundation of the entire plan of salvation. It was surely by design that the gematria for *"Blood of Jesus,"* αιμα Iησου, has the number value of 740.

The rock that the Israelites carried with them through the wilderness was not just an ordinary rock that they picked up along the way. It was a special rock that was sacred to them. There is evidence that it was the same rock on which Jacob laid his head the night that he had the vision of the ladder reaching from heaven to earth. That was the night that God confirmed the covenant with him, to bless all the families of the earth. When Jacob awoke that morning, he anointed the rock and gave it a name. He called it Bethel–the house of God. The account of this in Genesis 28:22 reads, *"And the stone shall become the house of God,"* והאבן יהיה בית אלהים. Its letter-numbers add to 592.

If we draw a square whose perimeter measures 592, and project its Golden Rectangle, its Golden Spiral will have a length of 355.2, and the long side of the rectangle will measure 148. The numbers tell the beautiful story of redemption through Jesus Christ, the River of Life that flows from the Wells of Salvation during earth's great antitypical Feast of Tabernacles.

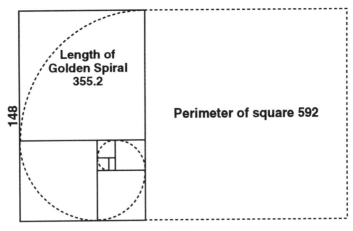

Length of
Golden Spiral
355.2

148

Perimeter of square 592

592   = And the stone shall become the House of God

3552 = The source of eternal salvation, αιτιος σωτηριας
αιωνιου, (Hebrews 5:9)

1480 = Christ, Χριστος

The drawing of water from the Wells of Salvation was what Jesus was referring to when he told the woman at the well, *"Whosoever drinks of the water that I shall give him shall never thirst; but the water that I shall give him shall be in him a fountain of water springing up into everlasting life."* (John 4:14)

As well as the drawing of water, there was another feature of the Temple service that took place during the Feast of Tabernacles which has its counterpart in Earth's Great Millennium. It was the illumination.

At the conclusion of the first day, four huge golden lampstands were lit. These were tall lampstands, or candelabra, each with four golden bowls against which rested four ladders. Four youths of priestly descent climbed the ladders, and with large pitchers of oil, filled each bowl. So brilliant was the light from these lampstands, that there came to be the saying, "There was not a court in Jerusalem that was not lit by it."

We usually think of the seven-branched candlesticks such as was used in the Tabernacle. But the lampstands used in the Temple, and for the Feast of Tabernacles were of a different design. It was this later design that Zechariah described, as was used in the second Temple (Zech. 4:3).

Around these great burning lamps a sacred dance took place, with men carrying flaming torches while they sang

These ritual seven-fold lamps have been found in several places in Israel, including Hazor, Dothan, and at Megiddo.

songs of praise to God. Harps, lutes, cymbals and trumpets accompanied the singing. It was a joyous and festive occasion.

The illumination had a two-fold significance. It was to remind them of the time when the Shekinah glory illuminated the first Temple; and it was to remind them of the promises of the coming of Messiah, the light of the world.

In Malachi 4:2 is a prophecy of the coming of Messiah, and it gives him a title that we might think is a play on words, but that similarity is only in English. In Hebrew it does not have this connotation. The prophecy reads, *"But unto you who fear My name, the Sun of Righteousness shall rise, and healing on His wings."* Yes, the Son, now is called the Sun, because he comes as the *"light of the world,"* and the healing rays from that illumination will bring life.

This quotation from Malachi adds to 2220. This triplet of twos is identified as the same one who gave the Apostle John the Revelation. There he called himself the Alpha and Omega. He was the one who came to earth and lived his childhood in the lowly town of Nazareth. He is the one who was called the firstborn from the dead, for death could not hold him. The numbers identify him:

2220 = But unto you who fear My name, the Sun of Righteousness shall rise, and healing on His wings, לכם יראי שמי שמש צדקה ומרפא בכנפיה וזרחה, (Mal. 4:2)

143

222 = Nazarene, $N\alpha\zeta\alpha\rho\eta\nu\varepsilon$

222 = Firstborn, בכר

222 = The Voice of God, קול אלהים, (In the New Testament he is called the Word of God.)

When the number 222 is used as the perimeter of a square, the Golden Rectangle that can be projected will have a long side of 55.5, and the Golden Spiral within it will have a length of 133.2

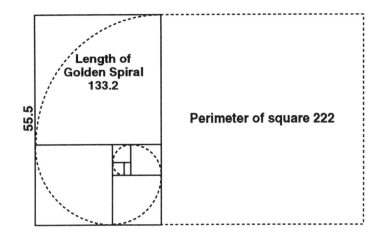

555 = Our Lord and His Christ, $K\upsilon\rho\iota\upsilon\upsilon$ $\eta\mu\omega\nu$ $\kappa\alpha\iota$ $\tau\upsilon\upsilon$ $X\rho\iota\sigma\tau\upsilon\upsilon$ $\alpha\upsilon\tau\upsilon\upsilon$, (This is prophetic of the time when Jesus begins his reign on David's Throne, Revelation 11:15)

1332 = Behold your King, $\iota\delta\upsilon\upsilon$ $\beta\alpha\sigma\iota\lambda\varepsilon\upsilon\varsigma$, (John 12:15)

When the Apostle John wrote of Jesus' triumphal entry into Jerusalem, just a few days before his death, he quoted the prophecy of Zechariah 9:9, *"Rejoice greatly, O daughter of Zion! Shout, O daughter of Jerusalem! Behold, your King comes to you! He is righteous and victorious; lowly and riding on an ass, even on a colt the foal of an ass."* John knew that this prophecy was speaking of Jesus, and when he saw Jesus riding on the donkey, he made the association in his mind– "This is what Zechariah prophesied." By riding into Jerusalem on the donkey, Jesus was making a statement: that he was the prophetic King. However, instead of setting up his kingdom, within a few days, he was put to death. John was left disappointed, for he had truly believed that Jesus was to be crowned king, and they would be freed from Roman rule.

Zechariah, however, saw the whole picture, and told of the conquering acts of this King. Acts which did not happen at the time when Jesus rode into Jerusalem on the donkey–they are future events, but just as sure of fulfillment. Zechariah said, *"And the battle bow shall be cut off, and He shall speak peace to the nations. And His dominion shall be from sea to sea and from the River to the ends of the earth."* He was prophesying of the Millennial kingdom of Christ, when the River of Life flows to the ends of the earth.

The interplay of the gematria between John and Zechariah is most interesting. When John wrote *"Behold your King,"* his statement added to 1332. When Zechariah wrote *"Behold your King,"* his statement multiplied to 6000. The relationship is indeed magnificent. Both come at the end of 6,000 years of man's experience on this earth, and at the beginning of the 7th thousand year period–the Millennium. The gematria of Zechariah identified the time, and the gematria of John identified the action.

And, as is shown by the above diagram, the Golden Spiral of 133.2 is linked with the square of 222, the Sun of Righteousness. He will indeed be the illumination that was pictured by the lighting of the lamps during the Feast of Tabernacles.

It was at the end of the first day of the Feast of Tabernacles that this ceremony of the lighting of the lamps occurred. It was a joyous celebration, and as the youths climbed the ladders and began to light the wicks we can imagine the shouts of joy and of song that followed as one by one the light became brighter until all were lit. The people began to dance with a festive abandon.

Reading about this joy of lighting the lamps, and being aware that sometimes added meaning is hidden in the gematria, I was curious about the gematria of the lampstands. To my amazement and delight, I found that the number value for *"lampstand,"* מנורה, is 301. It is the same as the gematria for *"fire,"* אש, thus the fire and the lamps both bore the same number, 301. It is also the gematria for *"Moon,"* σεληνη, or *"proclaim,"* קרא. But it was not only the number associated with illumination, but also with the water from the rock. *"He is the Rock"*

הצור adds to 301. This number is definitely associated with the great antitypical Feast of Tabernacles.

Out of curiosity, I multiplied 301 by the Golden Proportion, .618034, and found the tears running down my face as I looked at the answer on my calculator– it was 186. There are precisely 186 days from the day of the killing of the Passover Lamb to the end of the seventh day of the Feast of Tabernacles, bringing us to the beginning of the feast of the great 8th day, the octave. Jesus was the antitypical Passover Lamb who hung on the cross on a hill called Calvary. Calvary, $K\rho\alpha\nu\iota o\nu$, adds to 301. That same hill was also called Golgotha, $\Gamma o\lambda\gamma o\theta\alpha$, which adds to 186. Just before Jesus took his last breath, while hanging on that cruel cross, he said *"It is finished."* In Greek it is $\gamma\varepsilon\gamma o\nu\varepsilon\nu$, and it adds to 186.

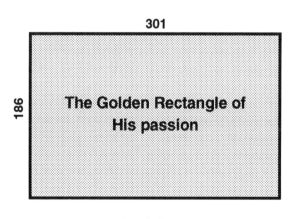

301 = Calvary
186 = Golgotha

The world-wide effects of the events of that day make themselves apparent in the geometry of the earth and its moon. Earth and moon orbit the sun as a *unit,* therefore we can place them together and take their combined measures. If we place the moon tangent to the earth (touching), and measure from the center of the earth to the center of the moon, we have combined the radii of both orbs. The distance is 5,040 miles. Let's draw a triangle on this combined radii.

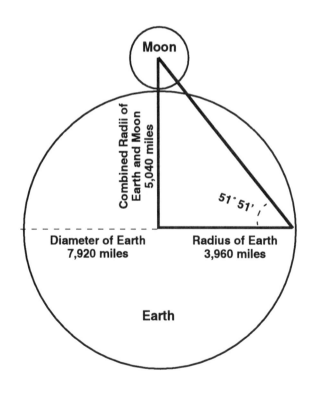

Now, we will change the dimensions of the triangle, keeping the same angles and the same proportions. Instead of 3,960 for the base of the triangle, we will use 186, the number obtained when adding the letter-numbers for the name Golgotha. Amazingly, the hypotenuse of the triangle will be 301, Calvary; and the height will be 236.8, which is the gematria for Jesus Christ. This is an earth-commensurate triangle, built upon the dimensions of earth and moon, and it bears the numbers of redemption.

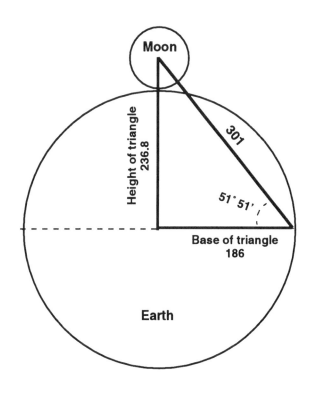

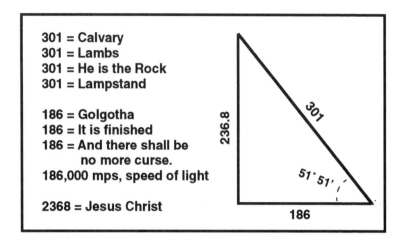

The above relationship of the numbers of redemption and the geometry of the earth is awesome! But there is more! The numbers that define the diameter and radius of the earth, and the combined radii of earth and moon, are sacred numbers in the gematria of the scriptures. They tell the story of salvation.

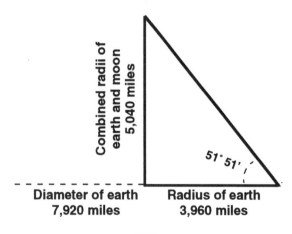

150

3,960 miles, radius of earth

396 = Salvation, הישועה

7,920 miles, diameter of earth

792 = Salvation, ישועות

5,040 miles, combined radii of earth and moon

5040 = The Kingdom of our Lord and His Christ,
βασιλεια Κυριου ημων και Χριστου αυτου,
(Revelation 11:15)

504 = The ransomed of the Lord shall return,
פדויי יהוה ישבון, (Isaiah 35:10)

504 = The house of David, סכת דויד, (Prophetic of the
reign of Jesus on the throne of David, Amos 9:11)

504 = The fountain of living water,
מקור מים חיים, (Jeremiah 2:13)

The place of salvation is the earth. These biblical statements concerning man's salvation and reconciliation bear
numbers that are the same as the measurements of the earth.
Jesus came from the heavenly courts, to earth, to be man's
redeemer. He came to pay the price for the sin of Adam,
and to set man free from the Adamic curse, death. His
death was by crucifixion. They nailed his hands and his
feet to a cross. David, in Psalm 22:16 spoke prophetically
of that momentous event. He said, *"They pierced my hands
and my feet."* Its letter-numbers add to 504. It was the
pivotal point in man's experience on this earth, for it

provided a hope of life, and of restitution, and of reconciliation. The above scriptural statements, each adding to 504, describe that future time–Earth's Great Millennium, the antitypical Feast of Tabernacles, the seventh, before the New Beginning, the Grand Octave.

When we use the function of multiplying the letter-numbers, the same story makes itself apparent. It speaks of salvation. The time is the seventh day; the place is the world; the means is through the blood of Christ presented on the "Mercy Seat"; the fulfillment is when He returns as Shiloh; and he brings peace to the earth. The seventh day is followed by the Grand Octave–Eternity. What a beautiful story is told in the numbers!

The following are by multiplication:

504 = Salvation, ישועתי

504 = Seventh day, יום השביעי

504 = World, עולם

504 = Mercy seat, *ιλαστηριov* (where atonement was made by the blood of Jesus, Hebrews 9:15)

504 = Saviour, מושיע

504 = Christ, *Χριστος*

504 = Until Shiloh comes, עד כי יבא שילה, (prophetic of the return of Jesus, Genesis 49:10)

504 = Peace, עלומי

504 = Eternity, עולם

Of all the feasts and celebrations that God gave to ancient Israel, the Feast of Tabernacles was the only one that had an octave.

By the end of the seventh day, the joy and excitement of the people reached its climax, but a hush fell over the crowds gathered in the streets, as the choir of the Levites began to sing the Hallel (consisting of Psalms 113 through 118), finishing with the song of thanks to God for his salvation:

> *"Open for me the gates of righteousness; I will enter and give thanks to the Lord. This is the gate of the Lord through which the righteous may enter. I will give you thanks, for you answered me; you have become my salvation.... This is the day the Lord has made; let us rejoice and be glad in it."*

Before the sun began to set, the people, who had been living in booths for seven days, began to return to their homes and prepare for the feast of the great 8th day. It was now 186 days since the first pilgrim festival of their year, the Passover. Their yearly festivals were coming to a close. There was one more day, yet to be celebrated–the feast of the great 8th day. It was sometimes called The Day of Conclusion, עצרת יום, (adds to 816).

The interplay of the numbers 1, 6 and 8 form an integral part of this final festival of the year. The counting of the days from Passover to the end of the seventh day of the Feast of Tabernacles was 186 days. The seventh day was called, האהרון של חג יום טוב, The Last Day of the Feast of Tabernacles, and its letter-numbers add to 681. This interplay of numbers is not unusual in the gematria of the scriptures. Numbers are often reversed or arranged in a different order, thus here, the number 186 and 681 are simply a reversal. Just as the Hebrew text reads from right to left, and the Greek text reads from left to right, so the numbers can also read either way, and are so used many times in the scriptures.

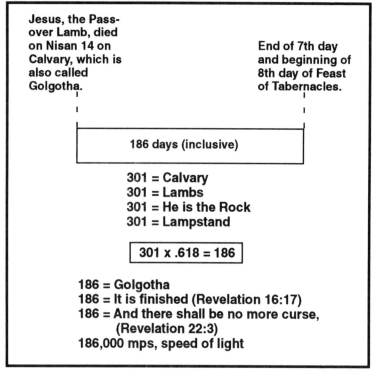

Jesus, the Passover Lamb, died on Nisan 14 on Calvary, which is also called Golgotha.

End of 7th day and beginning of 8th day of Feast of Tabernacles.

186 days (inclusive)

301 = Calvary
301 = Lambs
301 = He is the Rock
301 = Lampstand

$$301 \times .618 = 186$$

186 = Golgotha
186 = It is finished (Revelation 16:17)
186 = And there shall be no more curse, (Revelation 22:3)
186,000 mps, speed of light

The anagrams of 186 and the beginning of the Great Eighth Day

186,000 mps, Speed of Light
186 = It is finished (Revelation 16:17)
186 = And there shall be no more curse, (Rev. 22:3)
186 = Forever (Isa. 64:4)
186 = According to His image, (Gen. 5:3) (By the beginning of the Great 8th Day man will once again be in the image of God, just as Adam was before he sinned.)

681 = The Last Day of the Feast of Tabernacles
681 = Perfect (complete)

816 = The Day of Conclusion (8th day of Feast of Tabernacles)
816 = His Dominion

861 = Eternity
861 = Very early in the morning (the morning of that Great 8th Day)

168 = In His image (Gen. 1:27) (Man will again be in His image by the beginning of the Great 8th Day.)
1680 = Christ *(Χριστου)*
10608 = And he showed me a pure river of water of life, clear as crystal, proceeding out of the throne of God and of the Lamb. (Revelation 22:1) (This is a picture of the blessings of life in the Great 8th Day.)

.618 is the Golden Proportion
618 = The Lord shall be King over all the earth (Zechariah. 14:9)

The autumn before his death, Jesus came to Jerusalem to celebrate the Feast of Tabernacles. It was a bold move, because the Pharisees, who sought to kill him, were there also. And they did indeed, attempt to arrest him. But on the last day of the Feast, the Great Eighth Day, Jesus boldly stood up and proclaimed that he would be the fulfillment of the very thing that this great Feast was all about.

> *"On the last and greatest day of the Feast, Jesus stood and said in a loud voice, 'If anyone is thirsty, let him come to me and drink. Whoever believes in me, as the Scripture has said, streams of living water will flow from within him.'"* (John 7:37)

It probably sounded like a strange thing for him to say. And I doubt that those who heard him understood the message, for it was not until several decades later that John recorded the vision of Revelation that was given to him. And near the end of that vision, he described the Great Eighth Day, and said, *"Whoever is thirsty, let him come; and whoever wishes, let him take the free gift of the water of life,"* (Rev. 22:17)

John had recorded this, after he had seen the beautiful sight of a crystal clear river, flowing from beneath the throne of God. It was a healing river. It is one of the most beautiful scenes in the Bible, and I would like to quote it from the New International Version.

"Then the angel showed me the river of the water of life, as clear as crystal, flowing from the throne of God and of the Lamb, down the middle of the great street of the city. On each side of the river stood the tree of life, bearing twelve crops of fruit, yielding its fruit every month. And the leaves of the tree are for the healing of the nations. No longer will there be any curse (the curse that was placed on the earth when Adam sinned). *The throne of God and of the Lamb will be in the city, and his servants will serve him. They will see his face, and his name will be on their foreheads. There will be no more night. They will not need the light of a lamp or the light of the sun, for the Lord God will give them light. And they will reign for ever and ever* (Man will return to the condition of sonship with God and kingship over the earth, which Adam lost when he sinned)." (Revelation 22:1-5)[1]

In the 21st chapter of Revelation, John begins his description of the Great Eighth Day, in which he shows that the old order will pass away, and God's new order

---

1   Compare this with Ezekiel 47. It is the same beautiful picture of healing waters coming from the throne of God, and flowing to all mankind.

will be a living reality. He describes the New Jerusalem coming down and engulfing the earth. He said there would be no more tears, no more mourning, and no more death. *"He who was seated on the throne said, 'Behold I make all things new.'"* (Rev. 21:5) It is a magnificent promise. But its gematria is even more thrilling, because it tells the means by which this can all come about.

1958 = Behold, I make all things new.

It will be the magnificent gift of the Lord Jesus Christ. And if we divide 1958 by the Golden Proportion, we find the number of His name, 3168.

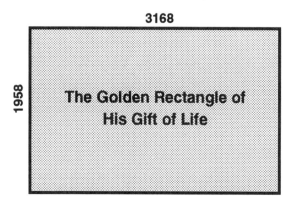

This precious gift of life, shown in the Golden Rectangle, is also magnificently displayed in the triangle that can be drawn on earth's diameter and the center of the moon. The proportions of that earth-commensurate triangle tell of the Lord Jesus Christ, and the "new earth" that he will provide for man. The same numbers in the Golden Rectangle of His Gift of Life, are in the dimensions of the triangle.

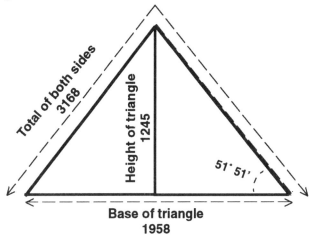

1245 = Mount Zion, Σιων ορει, (Hebrews 12:22)

This use of the term *"Mount Zion,"* is describing the New Jerusalem that comes down and fills the earth with its illumination.

> *"But you have come to Mount Zion, to the heavenly Jerusalem, the city of the living God."*

The prophet Isaiah saw, in vision, the same new heavens and new earth. It is man's New Beginning. He described it as a time when all men would know and worship their Maker.

"For as the new heavens and new earth, which I will make, shall remain before me, saith the Lord, so shall your seed and your name remain. And it shall come to pass, that from one new moon to another, and from one sabbath to another, shall all flesh come to worship before me, saith the Lord." (Isaiah 66:22, 23)

The *"new heavens and new earth,"* הֶחֳדָשִׁים וְהָאָרֶץ הַשָּׁמַיִם, multiplies to 248,832 (dropping the zeros). By the rules of gematria it is the same number as the mean circumference of the earth, which is 248,831.392 miles. How exciting to find, hidden in the number code, the assurance that this kingdom will be world-wide in its scope. Truly the New Jerusalem will encompass the whole earth with its blessings of life and peace.

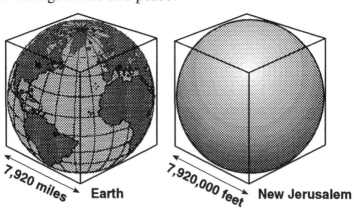

7,920 miles **Earth**

7,920,000 feet **New Jerusalem**

248,832 = New heavens and new earth
248,831.392 miles, circumference of earth.

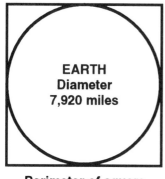

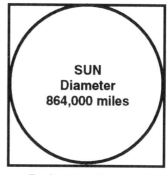

3168 = Lord Jesus Christ, *Κυριος Ιησους Χριστος*

3456 = Alpha and Omega, the Beginning and the End,
αλφα και το Ω η αρχη και το τελος,
(Revelation 21:6) (He is the Beginner and the New Beginner.)

792 = Salvation, ישועות

864 = New Earth, ארץ חדשה, (Isaiah 65:17, by multiplication)

By the end of the seven days of the Feast of Tabernacles–the end of Earth's Great Millennium–the light of the blessing of God will fill the earth. It will be brighter than the wonderful illumination of the lampstands during the seven days: even brighter than all seven days combined. Isaiah prophesied of that time, and used the illustration of the illumination during the Feast of Tabernacles. He was making a comparison, and a fitting one.

161

JESUS CHRIST: THE NUMBER OF HIS NAME

"The sunlight will be seven times brighter,
as the light of seven full days, when the Lord
binds up the bruises of his people and heals
the wounds he inflicted," (Isaiah 30:26)

The gematria for this light takes us all the way back to the beginning, before sin and disobedience entered. It bears the number 999. Nine is the number of completeness and wholeness. The first four words of the Bible (which are only two words in Hebrew) bear the number 999. It expressed a wholeness that had no need for anything to be added to it.

999 = In the beginning God, בראשית אלהים

999 = As the light of seven, כאור שבעת

The Grand Octave is complete. The New Beginning of the Great Eighth Day can commence. The plan of God for the salvation of man will be accomplished. Then will be fulfilled the beautiful statement of praise in Psalm 113:4, which adds to 1008–it bears the numbers of Beginning and New Beginning:

1008 = The Lord is high above all nations, and His glory above the heavens, (Psalm 113:4)

The prophet Habakkuk spoke of this ultimate relationship between God and man, when he said, *"The Lord is in His holy temple, let all the earth keep silence before Him."* What a beautiful picture of man, once again enjoying the sonship that he had lost at the beginning of the octave–now man will receive it again at the end of the octave and the beginning of eternity.

1080 = The Lord is in His holy temple, let all the earth keep silence before Him, (Hab. 2:20)

At the end of the Revelation, the angel said to John:

> *"No longer will there be any curse. The throne of God and of the Lamb will be in the city, and his servants will serve him. They will see his face, and his name will be on their foreheads. There will be no more night. They will not need the light of a lamp or the light of the sun, for the Lord God will give them light. And they shall reign for ever and ever."* (Rev. 22:3-5)

Yes they–all mankind who then will be in the relation of sonship with their Creator–will once again receive the dominion of earth that Adam lost. They will be kings, just as God had originally planned for his human family.

The Beginning and the New Beginning will have come

together in glorious completion. The number of Beginning, 1, and the number of New Beginning, 8, come together in the number that represents wholeness and completion, the number 9. $(1 + 8 = 9)$ It is the number that goes beyond the octave, and becomes the ultimate manifestation of the completeness of all the works of God.

The word *"perfection,"* in Hebrew, כליל, adds to 90 and multiplies to 18. It represents the completeness of all of God's works; the adding of the 1 and the 8, and bringing in the 9.

9 = New Earth, הארץ (Isaiah 66:22, by multiplication)

The description of that glorious New Earth was given to us by Paul in Ephesians 1:1-10 (Weymouth translation):

> *"God's merciful purpose for the government of the world when the times are ripe for it– the purpose which he has cherished in His own mind of restoring the whole creation to find its one head in Christ; yes, things in heaven and things on earth, to find their one Head in Him."*

9 = Jehovah-shammah (the Lord is there), יהוה שמה (by multiplication)

99 = Amen, $\alpha\mu\eta\nu$

999 = Glory to God, $\delta o\xi\alpha\nu\ \Theta\epsilon\omega$

Appendix I
JESUS CHRIST AND THE ELS CODE

The famed physicist, Sir Isaac Newton, left for us a legacy of the mechanics of the motion of our solar system and the force of gravity. He discovered and recorded many of the laws that we now know as accurate science. But the major thrust of his lifetime of study was not the motion of the planets, nor the phenomenon of gravity, nor the action of light; his true quest was to understand the Creator and the works of creation. Newton was a student of the Bible.

Newton's biographer, John Maynard Keynes, found the papers that Newton had packed up when he had retired from his position as provost at Cambridge University. They were in Newton's own handwriting. Keynes noted that most of the papers were not about physics, but about theology, and that Newton had felt the whole universe was a "cryptogram set by the Almighty."

Newton learned Hebrew, and searched for half a lifetime in an attempt to find the code that would reveal the past, present, and future events that God had foreordained in His great plan of salvation. But he died without ever finding the code that he knew must be there.

Newton lacked something that is available to us today– a computer.

In 1990, three mathematicians, Doron Witztum, Yoav Rosenberg, and Eliyahu Rips, of the Jerusalem College of

165

Technology and the Hebrew University, found what Newton had spent half a lifetime searching for. They called it the ELS code–Equidistant Letter Sequence. It reads words hidden by a skip sequence within the text. They developed software with which they could search for any name or event that might be encoded within the text of the Torah. The results were astonishing!

When word of this discovery reached investigative reporter, Michael Drosnin, formerly with the Washington Post and the Wall Street Journal, he felt it might be good for a story. He paid a visit to Rips.

Drosnin was skeptical. The whole concept seemed too far out to be real. However, after spending time with Rips, he became convinced that they were truly on to something exciting. Could this possibly be the code for which Newton had so diligently searched?

In the early autumn of 1994, Michael Drosnin, working with the software that had been developed for deciphering the code, came to a startling realization. Encoded within the original Hebrew text, was the message that Prime Minister Yitzhak Rabin would be assassinated, even giving the place and the date, Tel Aviv in the Hebrew year 5756. He was stunned! The event was yet future. Could he possibly warn Rabin, and save him from this fate?[1]

In September 1, 1994, Drosnin flew to Israel with a

---

1 Michael Drosnin, *The Bible Code,* Simon & Schuster, New York, p. 13

letter of warning for Rabin. It ended by saying, "You are in real danger."

On November 4, 1995 a shot rang out in Tel Aviv, and Prime Minister Yitzhak Rabin fell to the pavement. He was shot at close range by an assassin's bullet.

Reporter Drosnin was stunned! Up to that point he had still been a skeptic, but now he knew it was real.

With this evidence that shocked him into reality, he set anew to search the ELS code for any insight it may provide regarding the future. What he found is astounding!

Within the text of the Torah is a small 22-line scroll that is especially sacred. It is called the Mezuzah. This was written on a small scroll and placed into a wooden or metal container and attached to the doorposts of their houses. Every house in Israel had one, and many still do. This small scroll was also worn hanging from a chain around the neck. Its 22 lines obviously relate to the 22 letters of the Hebrew alphabet. It is a triple octave!

The words of this scroll were to be memorized, and talked of, and taught to their children. The instruction to Moses was:

> "...and these words which I am commanding you today shall be on your heart, and you shall repeat them to your sons, and shall speak of them as you sit in your house, and as you walk in the way, and as you are lying down, and as you are rising up, and

> *shall bind them for a sign on your hand;*
> *and they shall be for frontlets between your*
> *eyes. And you shall write them on the door-*
> *posts of your house and on your gates."*
> (Deut. 6:4-9)

Very obviously, God wanted his people to remember the words of this scroll. It was to be a part of their daily lives, and of their every act and thought. Its primary message was that they were to *"Love the Lord your God."* And the whole text was an admonition to hear and consider *"these words."*

252 = These words, דברי אלה

576 = To love the Lord your God, לאהבה את יהוה אלהיכם

The surface text does not appear to have any reference to time. However, the ELS code finds years on the Hebrew calendar encoded within the text. And it is remarkable, that the years that Drosnin found encoded in the Mezuzah, are the years indicated by the two numbers, 252 and 576. They are the Hebrew years 5760 and 5766. (5766 is 2,520 days, or 6 years and 11 months after 5760.)

And if we multiplied the Hebrew letters in the above text, it would produce 240 and 180 respectively. They are not random numbers. Multiply them (240 x 180) and the product is 25,920, which is the number of years in the Great Year, the length of time it takes the sun to progress through all twelve signs of the Zodiac.

Drosnin found the years 5760 and 5766 crossed by other words that indicated the events of those years. Encoded into the text he found the words "World War" and "Armageddon."

The Hebrew year 5760 begins on September 11, 1999 and continues through to the autumn of 2000. We have already noted the importance of the number 576 in the gematria of the scriptures. Zechariah 14–the prophecy of the second coming and Earth's Great Millennium–uses the term *"The Lord my God and all his holy ones"* when speaking of that long awaited return. The letter-numbers of its text add to 576. It appears to be identifying the time of his return. If so, then the seven years (6 years 11 months) following would fulfill the prophecy of Daniel 9:27 regarding the final 7 years of tribulation, ending in Armageddon, bringing us to the Hebrew year 5766, or our year 2006. But the gematria does not paint a picture of Armageddon, rather it tells of the Prince of Peace and the glory of the Messiah in his Kingdom.

The following are by multiplication:

576 = Messiah the Prince, משיח נגיד (Daniel 9:25)

576 = His glory, כבודו (Isaiah 6:3)

576 = He shall appear in his glory, נראה בכבודו (Psa. 102:16)

576 = His Kingdom, מלכות (Daniel 7:27, prophetic of Messiah's return)

169

JESUS CHRIST: THE NUMBER OF HIS NAME

The gematria 576 appears to be describing the return of Messiah and the time when he will begin his reign on David's throne–the event spoken of in Revelation 11:15:

> *"The seventh angel sounded; and there were great voices in heaven, saying, The kingdoms of this world are become the kingdom of our Lord, and of his Christ; and he shall reign for ever and ever."*

Yet, Drosnin found both 5760 and 5766 encoded into the Mezuzah, crossed by "World War" and "Armageddon." And in another text, he found 5766 crossed by "Great Earthquake." In Revelation, the Great Earthquake that is spoken of as happening at the time of Armageddon uses the Greek words $\mu\epsilon\gamma\alpha\sigma\ \sigma\epsilon\iota\sigma\mu\sigma\varsigma$, which adds to 974. If we multiply these three digits, the product is 252. This is a period of seven years ($7 \times 360 = 2520$). These seven years that follow the return of the Messiah are spoken of as years of tribulation, at the end of which is the final battle–Armageddon. Thus adding 2520 days to the Hebrew year 5760 brings us to the Hebrew year 5766, just as Drosnin observed in the ELS code.

And indeed an earthquake, as well as the return of the Lord, appears to be described in Zechariah 14.

> *"On that day his feet will stand on the Mount of Olives, east of Jerusalem, and the Mount*

of Olives will be split in two from east to west...and you will flee as you fled from the earthquake in the days of Uzziah...then the Lord my God will come, and all the holy ones with him."

The appearance of the Hebrew years 5760 and 5766 in the ELS code is in complete harmony with the gematria that was also encoded into the text. The evidence is truly mind-boggling! It speaks loudly of a Master Mathematician and a Master Cryptographer, who not only gave us the surface meaning of the plain text, but also encoded into that same text, his hidden messages, both in the ELS code and in gematria. It is beyond our human comprehension that such a thing could be done. Surely it would take the mind of the Creator.

When I first heard of the ELS code, I was skeptical, as just about everyone was. I remember, 30 years ago, when I first heard about gematria, I was skeptical. I feared that it was something of the occult, or a pseudo science, and something to be avoided when dealing with the word of God. However, during these many years of studying the gematria of the Hebrew and Greek texts, the evidence has been overwhelming. There is no way it could be some grand colossal coincidence. There is no way that man could have knowingly put it there, because the sixty six books of the Bible were written by men, most of whom did not know each other, over a period of more than 2,000 years. How could a consistent pattern of numbers, all telling the same story, have been encoded into the text?

As I pondered the magnificent implications of the existence of both codes, I wondered if, by any chance, there was indeed a third code, combining the ELS with gematria. But how would I find out? It would require the necessary software. All my work with gematria has been done with a simple hand-held calculator. I do not have software for working with gematria. Nor do I have software for working with ELS. Yet, my curiosity drove me to attempt it by hand, with my calculator.

Where would I begin? What would be the most obvious text with which to experiment? It had appeared, over the years, that the name Lord Jesus Christ had taken the prominent place in the study of gematria, thus my mind was led to the most famous prophecy concerning his coming to earth. It is the text that we read every Christmas concerning the promise of his birth.

> *"For unto us a child is born, unto us a son is given, and the government shall be on his shoulder; and his name shall be called Wonderful, Counselor, the Mighty God, the Everlasting Father, the Prince of Peace."*
> (Isaiah 9:6)

I wondered if the skip sequence and the gematria, combined, would reveal anything of importance. But what skip-sequence to use? The number 7 seemed like an appropriate number, because it relates to the octave. If 7 did not work, the next one I would try would be 8, the complete octave and the new beginning.

With calculator in hand, I pulled out every seventh Hebrew letter in the text, then added their number equivalents. As I punched the final "plus" on the calculator, my eyes filled with tears as I read the answer–888. Surely it must be a mistake! I counted carefully and added them again. And again the answer was 888. The seven-skip sequence, combined with the gematria of this most famous prophecy of the birth of Jesus, added to the number of his name.

888 = Jesus, $Iησους$

The tears were running down my face. But I still had doubts. It must have been a coincidence, I thought. I must try another text to see if it really works.

With my Hebrew text open to Isaiah, I turned a few pages and my attention was directed to chapter 11, the first verse. This would be a good one to try, I thought, because it tells of him being the Branch out of David's root. Using the 7-skip sequence, I pulled out every seventh letter and assigned their number equivalents, then began adding them. As I punched the last "plus" on the calculator and looked at the answer, a joy filled my whole being. There before me were the three 8s again. The total was 888! Both texts, prophetic of the coming of Jesus as the babe of Bethlehem, of the lineage of David, possessing great power and wisdom, and the spirit of the Lord, the one who will be ruler on David's throne, the one called the Prince of Peace–both texts have hidden within them, the combination of the ELS code and gematria, pointing to Jesus, the great 888. Let me share them with you. They are beautiful! (Remember, Hebrew reads from right to left.)

Isaiah 9:6

"For unto us a child is born, unto us a son is given, and the government shall be on his shoulder; and his name shall be called Wonderful, Counselor, the Mighty God, the Everlasting Father, the Prince of Peace."

כי ילד ילד לנו בן נתן לנו ותהי
400   50   30

המשרה על שכמו ויקרא שמו
6   6   5

פלא יועץ אל גבור אבי עד
1   90

שר שלום
300

30 + 50 + 400 + 5 + 6 + 6 + 90 + 1 + 300 = 888

Jesus = 888

Isaiah 11:1

"And a shoot will come up from the stump of Jesse; from his roots a Branch will bear fruit. The spirit of the Lord will rest on him— the spirit of wisdom and of understanding, the spirit of counsel and of power, the spirit of knowledge and of the fear of the Lord— and he will delight in the fear of the Lord."

ויצא חטר מגזע ישי ונצר משרשיו
200   10   200

יפרה ונחה עליו רוח יהוה רוח
6   10   5

חכמה ובינה רוה עצה וגבורה
3   200   40

רוח דעת ויראת יהוה והריחו
5   1   8

ביראת יהוה
200

200 + 10 + 200 + 5 + 10 + 6 +
40 + 200 + 3 + 8 + 1 + 5 + 200 = 888

Jesus = 888

Not having the necessary software, I could not further pursue the quest. However, one day, while reading the book of Malachi, I was curious about the addition of the text, beginning with the 3rd chapter, because it appears to be telling of the return of Jesus. I added the letter-numbers of the text and was positively delighted to find that their total was 5184. It was a number that I knew was important in the gematria of the scriptures, and I knew that a pentagon with sides of 5,184 had a total perimeter of 25,920, which is the number of years required for the sun to progress through all twelve signs of the Zodiac. And I also knew that $9 \times 576 = 5184$. Thus, finding the number 5184 in this text attracted my special attention.

5184 = Behold, I am sending my messenger, and he shall prepare the way before me. And the Lord whom you seek shall suddenly come to his Temple, even the Messenger of the Covenant, in whom you delight. Behold he comes.

I wondered if a skip sequence would reveal any additional information that might be hidden within the text. But what skip sequence to use! Since this text appeared to be talking about the return of the Lord, and its total by addition was nine times the number that appeared to relate to the year of his return, 576, I decided to try a skip 9 sequence.

After pulling out every ninth Hebrew letter in the text,

and adding their total, I was overjoyed to find it to be the number 586. It was the number for *"Jerusalem"* in the Hebrew text. It was also the number for *"trumpet."* The connection was obvious. His return is prophesied to be with the sound of a trumpet (probably symbolic of some means of announcement), and his return is also stated to be in Jerusalem.

586 = Jerusalem, ירושלם

586 = Trumpet, שופר

The inter-relationship of the numbers seems beyond the reach of coincidence. The number 5184 for the text regarding his return, and the skip sequence revealing the number 586, is in complete harmony with the phrase that God used when referring to the city of Jerusalem. He called it *"My Holy Jerusalem,"* Its letter-numbers multiply to 5184.

5184 = My Holy Jerusalem, קדשי ירושלם

And the pentagon whose sides are 5,184 has a perimeter of 25,920, which is the multiplication of the letter-numbers in *"The heart of Jerusalem"* as used in Isaiah 40:2.

2592 = The heart of Jerusalem, לב ירושלם

The text is a beautiful one, for it tells of the time coming when Jerusalem will be at peace.

> *"Comfort, O comfort my people, says your God. Speak lovingly to the heart of Jerusalem–yea, cry to her that her warfare is done, that her iniquity is pardoned; for she has received of Jehovah's hand double for all her sins.... the glory of the Lord shall be revealed, and all flesh shall see it together, for the mouth of the Lord of Hosts has spoken. "* (Isaiah 40:1-4)

Appendix II
JESUS CHRIST AND THE NUMBER 37

When we think of the Beginning and the New Beginning, we must also think of the Beginner and the New Beginner. They are inseparable in the work of creation and restoration. The Apostle John said of the Son, *"All things were made by him, and without him was nothing made."* Yet many scriptures speak of the Father as the Creator. Harmony comes in realizing that Jesus, the Son, was the active agent of the Father in the works of Creation In fact, the names and titles of the one are also often used for the other–and sometimes both are called by one name, such as *Elohim,* which is a plural Hebrew word that is often used for both the Father and the Son. Therefore it is not surprising that the number 37, which is basic to the names and titles of Jesus, is also basic to the names and titles of the Father.

The use of the number 37 in the gematria of their names is truly astounding. It carries us far beyond the realm of coincidence, and displays a plan and a pattern, encoded into the written word by a mind far superior to anything that man can devise. So many of the names and titles of both the Father and the Son are multiples of 37 that it commands our attention. The list below is certainly not exhaustive. These are merely the ones that I have observed, without the use of computer software with which to search for them.

37

37 = God, אלהא, (Daniel 4:2)

37 = Only Son, היחיד

37 = Power, אול

370 = Everlasting righteousness, צדקלעולם, (Psa. 119:142)

370 = He lives, שכן, (Isaiah 33:5)

37 = Only begotten, יחידה

370 = He rules, משל, (Psalm 66:7)

370 = God is my King of old, אלהים מלכי מקדם, (Psalm 74:12)

370 = The Breaker, פרץ, (Micah 2:13)

37 = Glory, הכבוד

370 = Whole, שלם

370 = Whole, ολος

370 = To make restitution, שלם

37 = Truth, לוא

37 = All glorious, כבודה

370 = The pleasure of Jehovah shall prosper in His hands, וחפץ יהוה בידו יצלח, (Isaiah 53:10, prophetic of Jesus.)

370 = He shall rule wisely, ישכיל, (Isaiah 52:13, prophetic of Jesus as King on David's throne.)

370 = He has founded the earth, ארץ יסדה, (Amos 9:6)

37 = Like a fish, כדגי, (The symbol of Christianity has always been the fish.)

370 = My Messiah, במשיחי, (Psalm 105:15)

370 = The way everlasting, צדק לעולם, (Psalm 119:142)

370 = Peace, שלם

370 = He is humble and riding (on an ass,) ורכב
הוא עני, (Zechariah 9:9, prophetic of Jesus'
triumphal entry into Jerusalem four days before
his death.)

370 = A shadow from the heat, צל מחרב, (Isaiah 25:4,
prophetic of Jesus during his reign on David's
throne.)

370 = To reign, משל

37 x 2 = 74

74 = A great God, אל גדול, (Psalm 95:3)

74 = Their Redeemer, גאלם,(Jeremiah 50:34)

740 = Judge of all the earth, השפט כל הארץ, (Gen. 18:25)

740 = Circle, κυκλος

740 = Creation, κτισις

74 = Foundation, יסד

74 = Everlasting, עד

740 = You have laid the foundation of the earth,
הארין יסדת, (Psalm 102:25)

740 = Blood of Jesus, αιμα Ιησου, (I John 1:7)

37 x 3 = 111

111 = Wonderful, אלפ, (Isaiah 9:6, prophetic of Jesus)

111 = The Most High, עליא, (Daniel 4:32)

1110 = Only Son, υιος μονος, (John 3:16)

1110 = The blood of Jesus, το αιμα Ιησου, (I John 1:7)

111 = Son of the Living God, בני אל חי, (Hosea 1:10)

111 = Lord of all, אדון כל, (Proverbs 17:8)

37 x 4 = 148

1480 = Christ, $X\rho\iota\sigma\tau\sigma\varsigma$

1480 = Son of God, $\upsilon\iota\sigma\varsigma$ $K\upsilon\rho\iota\sigma\varsigma$

148 = The Most High, אלהא עליא, (Daniel 4:2)

1480 = Kingdom of God, $\beta\alpha\sigma\iota\lambda\epsilon\iota\alpha\nu$ $\alpha\upsilon\tau\sigma\upsilon$, (Matt. 6:33)

148 = Passover, פסח, (Jesus was the Passover Lamb)

148 = Way, מעגלה, (Jesus said *"I am the Way."*)

37 x 5 = 185

185 = Rabbi, σ $\rho\alpha\beta\beta\iota$

185 = Glory, $\delta\sigma\xi\alpha\nu$

1850 = The strong man, $\tau\sigma\nu$ $\iota\sigma\chi\upsilon\rho\sigma\nu$, (Matthew 12:29, representing Jesus.)

37 x 6 = 222

222 = The Voice of God, קול אלהים, (Deut. 4:33)

2220 = I am Alpha and Omega, $\epsilon\gamma\omega$ $A\lambda\phi\alpha$ $\kappa\alpha\iota$ $\Omega\mu\epsilon\gamma\alpha$

222 = The Lord is my Rock and my Shield, יהוה עזי ומגני, (Psalm 28:7)

222 = Nazarene, $N\alpha\zeta\alpha\rho\eta\nu\epsilon$

2220 = Unto you that fear my name shall the Sun of Righteousness arise with healing in his wings, וזרחה לכם יראי שמי שמש צדקה ומרפא בכנפיה, (Malachi 4:2)

37 x 7 = 259

259 = Kingdom, $\beta\alpha\sigma\iota\lambda\epsilon\iota\alpha$

2590 = Only Son, Christ, $\upsilon\iota o\varsigma \mu o\nu o\varsigma X\rho\iota\sigma\tau o\varsigma$

2590 = Of the seed of David, $o\tau\iota \epsilon\kappa \tau o\upsilon \sigma\pi\epsilon\rho\mu\alpha\tau o\varsigma$ $\Delta\alpha\upsilon\iota\delta$, (John 7:42)

259 = The glory of the Lord shall be forever, יהי כבוד יהוה לעולם, (Psalm 104:31)

37 x 8 = 296

296 = The Rock, צור

296 = God, צור

296 = Only begotten, $\mu o\nu o\gamma\epsilon\nu\eta$

2960 = Son of Man, $\upsilon\iota o\varsigma \tau o\upsilon \alpha\nu\theta\rho\omega\pi o\upsilon$, (Matthew 8:20)

296 = The Lord reigns forever, יהוה ימלך לעלם, (Ex. 15:18)

296 = He shall appear in His glory, נראה בכבודו, (Psalm 102:16)

296 = The beautiful Branch of Jehovah, צמח יהוה לצבי, (Isaiah 4:2)

37 x 9 = 333

333 = Thy throne O God is forever, כסאך אלהים עולם, (Psalm 45:6, prophetic of Jesus as king on David's throne.)

3330 = Lord of lords, $K\upsilon\rho\iota o\varsigma \tau\omega\nu \kappa\upsilon\rho\iota\omega\nu$

3330 = The will of God in Christ Jesus, $\theta\epsilon\lambda\eta\mu\alpha \Theta\epsilon o\upsilon \epsilon\nu$ $X\rho\iota\sigma\tau\omega I\eta\sigma o\upsilon$, (I Thess. 5:18)

333 = He is like a fire, הוא כאש, (Malachi 3:2, prophetic of Jesus.)

37 x 11 = 407

407 = Lord of all the earth, אדון כל הארץ, (Joshua 3:13)

407 = Ark, תבה, (Noah's Ark was typical of our salvation through Christ.)

37 x 12 = 444

4440 = The Lord Christ, τω Κυριω Χριστω, (Col. 3:24)

4440 = Christ, the Son of Man, Χριστος υιος του ανθρωπου

4440 = Behold He cometh with clouds, ιδου ερχεται μετα των νεφελων, (Rev. 1:7)

444 = Atonement, καταλλαγην, (Romans 5:11)

37 x 13 = 481

481 = The beginning (or the genesis of Christ), η γενεσις, (Matthew 1:1)

37 x 14 = 518

518 = Sun, ηλιου, (Mark 16:2)

518 = The Door, η θυρα, (John 10:9, Jesus said *"I am the Door."*

5180 = The Father sent the Son to be the Saviour of the world, ο πατηρ απεσταλ κεν τον υιον σωτηρα του κοσμου, (I John 4:14)

37 x 15 = 555

5550 = Our Lord and His Christ, $Kυριου ημων και του$
$Χριστου αυτου,$ (Revelation 11:15)

555 = He will build the Temple of Jehovah, את היכל יהוה
ובנה, (Zechariah 6:12, prophetic of Christ)

555 = Lord of Hosts, ליהוה צבאות, (I Samuel 1:3)

37 x 16 = 592

592 = Godhead, $Θεοτης$

592 = The Lord of heaven, מרא שמיא, (Daniel 5:23)

592 = Holiness, $αγιοτης$

592 = The Holy One of Jacob, קדוש יעקב, (Isaiah 29:23)

37 x 17 = 629

629 = The true Word, $αληθης Λογος$

37 x 18 = 666

666 = Jehovah God that created the heavens, בורא השמים
האל יהוה, (Isaiah 42:5)

666 = He hath made the earth, עשה ארץ, (Jeremiah 10:12)

666 = Your judgments are as the light, משפטיך אור,
(Hosea 6:5)

666 = Your great and fearful name, שמך גדול ונורא,
(Psalm 99:3)

666 = Excellency, יתרון

666 = Let there be lights, יהי מארת, (Genesis 1:14)

37 x 19 = 703

703 = The God of Israel, ο Θεος Ισραηλ

703 = The Holy one of Israel, ο αγιος Ισραηλ

703 = The God of David, Θεος Δαυιδ

37 x 21 = 777

777 = The man child, τον αρσενα, (Revelation 12:13)

777 = I (Jehovah) have raised him (Jesus) up,
אנכי העירתהו, (Isaiah 45:13)

777 = He is exalted in power and justice, שגיא כח ומשפט,
(Job 37:23)

777 = Love of God, αγαπης Θεου, (Romans 8:39)

777 = On the Mount of Olives (where his feet will stand
at his return), על הר הזיתים, (Zechariah 14:4)

37 x 22 = 814

814 = The powerful Word (of God), ο λογος ενεργης,
(Hebrews 4:12)

814 = God, Θεω, (Mark 10:27)

814 = His throne as the sun before me, כסאו כשמש נגדי,
(Psalm 89:36)

37 x 24 = 888

888 = Jesus, Ιησους

888 = The Founder, ο οικιστης

888 = I am the life, ειμι η ζωη

888 = Thou Lord art exalted forever, מרום לעלם יהוה
אתה, (Psalm 92:8)

888 = Salvation of our God, ישועת אלהינו, (Isaiah 52:10)

888 = I am Jehovah I change not, אני יהוה לא שניתי, (Malachi 3:6)

888 = A Priest with Urim and Thumim, לאורים ולתמים כהן, (Ezra 2:63, prophetic of Jesus)

888 = And the light dwells in Him, ונהירא עמה שרא, (Daniel 2:22)

888 = The heavens declare the glory of God, כבוד אל השמים מספרים, (Psalm 19:1)

8880 = An ark, in which a few, that is eight souls were saved through water, κιβωτου εις ην ολιγοι τουτ εστιν οκτω ψυχαι διεσωθησαν δι υδατος, (I Peter 3:20, The ark pictured salvation through Jesus Christ.)

8880 = Behold, a virgin shall conceive and bear a son, and they will call his name Emmanuel, which being interpreted is God with us, ιδου η παρθενος εν γαστρι εξει και τεξεται υιον και καλεσουσιν ονομα αυτου Εμμανουηλ ο εστιν μεθερμηνευομενον μεθ ημων Θεος, Matthew 1:23)

37 x 26 = 962

962 = Godhead, Θεοτητος, (Col. 2:9)

962 = Thou art clothed with honor and majesty, הוד והדר לבשת, (Psalm 104:1)

JESUS CHRIST: THE NUMBER OF HIS NAME

37 x 27 = 999

999 = In the beginning God, בראשית אלהים, (Gen. 1:1)

999 = Glory of God, $\delta o \xi \alpha v \Theta \epsilon \omega$, (Romans 4:20)

999 = A door of hope, פתחתקוה, (Hosea 2:15)

37 x 28 = 1036

1036 = God and the Lamb, $o \Theta \epsilon o \varsigma \kappa \alpha \iota \tau o \alpha \rho v \iota o v$,
(Revelation 21:23, The glory of God did lighten it,
and the Lamb is the light thereof.)

1036 = I am the resurrection, $\epsilon \iota \mu \iota \eta \alpha v \alpha \sigma \tau \alpha \sigma \iota \varsigma$,
(John 11:15)

1036 = The resurrection, $\eta \epsilon \xi \alpha v \alpha \sigma \tau \alpha \sigma \iota \varsigma$, (Phil. 3:1)

37 x 29 = 1073

1073 = The God of the earth, $o \Theta \epsilon o \varsigma \tau \eta \varsigma \gamma \eta \varsigma$,
(Genesis 24:3, from the Septuagint)

37 x 31 = 1147

1147 = The will of God, $\theta \epsilon \lambda \eta \mu \alpha \tau o \varsigma \Theta \epsilon o v$,
(Romans 15:32)

37 x 32 = 1184

1184 = Chief cornerstone, $\alpha \kappa \rho o \gamma \omega v \iota \alpha \iota o v$, (I Peter 2:6)

1184 = Throne of God, $\theta \rho o v o v \Theta \epsilon o v$, (Revelation 22:1)

1184 = In a different form, $\epsilon v \epsilon \tau \epsilon \rho \alpha \mu o \rho \phi \eta$, (Mark 16:12,
Jesus, after his resurrection, appeared
"in a different form" to his disciples on the road
to Emmaus.)

37 x 33 = 1221

1221 = Wonderful, $\Theta\alpha\nu\mu\alpha\sigma\tau\sigma\varsigma$, (Isaiah 9:6, the prophetic name of Jesus from the Septuagint.)

1221 = Carcass, $\pi\tau\omega\mu\alpha$, (Matthew 24:28, the humanity of Jesus as man's ransom price.)

1221 = His feet shall stand in that day on the Mount of Olives, עמדו רגליו ביום ההוא על הר הזיתים, (Zechariah 14:4, prophetic of the return of Jesus with his saints.)

1221 = Holy Master, $\delta\epsilon\sigma\pi\sigma\tau\eta\varsigma$ o $\alpha\gamma\iota\sigma\varsigma$, (Revelation 6:10)

37 x 36 = 1332

1332 = Alpha, Omega (first and last), $\alpha\lambda\phi\alpha$ ω

1332 = True God, $\alpha\lambda\eta\theta\omega\varsigma$ $\Theta\epsilon\sigma\varsigma$

1332 = Behold your King, $\iota\delta\sigma\upsilon$ $\beta\alpha\sigma\iota\lambda\epsilon\upsilon\varsigma$, (John 12:15)

37 x 37 = 1369

1369 = Image of God, $\epsilon\iota\kappa\omega\nu$ $\Theta\epsilon\sigma\upsilon$, (II Corinthians 4:4)

1369 = The God of life, o $\Theta\epsilon\sigma\varsigma$ $\zeta\omega\eta\varsigma$

1369 = The Son of David (Jesus), o $\upsilon\iota\sigma\upsilon$ $\Delta\alpha\upsilon\iota\delta$, (Matthew 1:1)

37 x 38 = 1406

1406 = Messiah the Son, $M\epsilon\sigma\sigma\iota\alpha\varsigma$ o $\upsilon\iota\sigma\varsigma$

37 x 39 = 1443

1443 = The Word of the Lord, o $\lambda\sigma\gamma\sigma\varsigma$ $K\upsilon\rho\iota\sigma\upsilon$

1443 = The peace of God, η $\epsilon\iota\rho\eta\nu\eta$ $\tau\sigma\upsilon$ $\Theta\epsilon\sigma\upsilon$, (Phil. 4:7)

JESUS CHRIST: THE NUMBER OF HIS NAME

37 x 42 = 1554

1554 = Only Word of the Father, μονος λογος πατρος

1554 = My beloved Son, υιον μου αγαπητον,
(Luke 20:13)

1554 = We have found the Messiah, ευρηκαμεν τον
Μεσσιαν, (John 1:41)

37 x 43 = 1591

1591 = Spirit of life, πνευμα ζωης

1591 = I am the Good Shepherd, εγω ειμι ο ποιμην ο
καλος, (John 10:11)

37 x 45 = 1665

1665 = The mouth of God, στοματος Θεου, (Matt. 4:4)

37 x 47 = 1739

1739 = Christ Kingdom, Χριστος βασιλεια

37 x 48 = 1776

1776 = Lord of the Sabbath, Κυριος σαββατου,
(Mark 2:28)

1776 = River of life, ποταμος ζωης, (Revelation 22:1)

1776 = The Lamb in the midst of the throne, οτι αρνιον
ανα μεσον θρονου, (Revelation 7:17)

1776 = I am the root and the offspring of David, εγω ειμι
η ριζα και γενος Δαυιδ, (Revelation 22:16)

37 x 49 = 1813

1813 = Lord of hosts, *Κυριος σαβαωθ,* (Romans 9:29)

37 x 52 = 1924

1924 = The God of the Universe, *ο Θεου του κοσμος*

1924 = Day of the Lord, *ημερα του Κυριου,* (I Cor. 1:8)

37 x 54 = 1998

1998 = The son of the virgin, *ο υιος εκ της παρθενου*

1998 = This same Jesus, *ουτος ο Ιησους,* (Acts 2:11)

37 x 55 = 2035

2035 = Christ in you, *Χριστος εν υμιν,* (Col. 1:27)

2035 = Wisdom of God, *σοφια του Θεου,* (Ephesians 3:10 and I Cor. 1:24, used as a metaphor of Jesus.)

2035 = The righteousness of God, *η δικαιοσυνη του Θεου,* (II Peter 1:1 and Romans 10:3, used as a metaphor of Jesus.)

37 x 56 = 2072

2072 = The Alpha, the Omega, *το αλφα το ω,* (Revelation 1:18, the first and the last.)

37 x 59 = 2183

2183 = The right hand of God, $\delta\varepsilon\xi\iota\omega\nu$ $\tauo\upsilon$ $\Theta\varepsilono\upsilon$, (Acts 7:55)

2183 = Head over all things to the church, $\kappa\varepsilon\phi\alpha\lambda\eta$ $\upsilon\pi\varepsilon\rho$ $\pi\alpha\nu\tau\alpha$ $\tau\eta$ $\varepsilon\kappa\kappa\lambda\eta\sigma\iota\alpha$, (Ephesians 1:22)

37 x 61 = 2257

2257 = Gospel of Christ, $\varepsilon\upsilon\alpha\gamma\gamma\varepsilon\lambda\iotao\nu$ $X\rho\iota\sigma\tauo\upsilon$

2257 = Noah's Ark, $\kappa\iota\beta\omega\tauo\varsigma$ $N\omega\varepsilon$, (An illustration of salvation through Christ.)

37 x 62 = 2294

2294 = His life (Christ's), $\tau\eta$ $\zeta\omega\eta$ $\alpha\upsilon\tauo\upsilon$, (Rom. 5:10)

37 x 63 = 2331

2331 = This Jesus hath God raised up, $\tauo\nu$ $I\eta\sigmao\upsilon\nu$ $\alpha\nu\varepsilon\sigma\tau\eta\sigma\varepsilon\nu$ o $\Theta\varepsilono\varsigma$, (Acts 2:32)

37 x 64 = 2368

2368 = Jesus Christ, $I\eta\sigmao\upsilon\varsigma$ $X\rho\iota\sigma\tauo\varsigma$

2368 = Him for whom are all things, $\alpha\upsilon\tau\omega$ $\delta\iota$ $o\nu$ $\tau\alpha$ $\pi\alpha\nu\tau\alpha$, (Hebrews 2:10)

2368 = The man whose name is The Branch, He shall grow up out of His place, and He shall build the Temple of Jehovah, שמו ומתחתיו יצמח ובנה את היכל יהוה איש צמח, (Zechariah 6:12)

37 x 66 = 2442

2442 = The Son of God, τη υιου του Θεου, (Gal. 2:20)

2442 = Jesus, the name given by the angel, Ιησους το κληθεν υπο αγγελου, (Luke 2:21)

37 x 69 = 2553

2553 = Name of the only begotten Son of God, ονομα μονογενους υιου Θεου, (John 3:18)

37 x 72 = 2664

2664 = The Lord God is one Lord, Κυριος Θεος εις εστιν Κυριος, (Mark 12:29)

37 x 73 = 2701

2701 = The grace of Christ, χαριτι Χριστου, (Gal. 1:6)

2701 = In the beginning God created the heaven and the earth, בראשית אלהים ברא את השמים ואת הארץ , Genesis 1:1)

37 x 75 = 2775

2775 = The Prince of Life, τον αρχηγον της ζωης, Acts 3:15)

37 x 76 = 2812

2812 = His eternal power and Godhead, η αιδιος αυτου δυναμις και Θειοτης, (Romans 1:20)

2812 = Blood of Christ, αιματι του Χριστου, (Eph. 2:13)

2812 = Eternal redemption, αιωνιαν λυτρωσιν, (Heb. 9:12)

37 x 91 = 3367

3367 = Father of spirits, πατρι των πνευματων,
(Hebrews 12:9)

37 x 92 = 3404

3404 = His divine power, της θειας δυναμεως αυτου,
(II Peter 1:3)

37 x 93 = 3441

3441 = The riches of His glory, τον πλουτον της δοξης
αυτου, (Romans 9:23)

3441 = A High Priest after the order of Melchizedek,
αρχιερευς κατα την ταξιν Μελχισεδεκ,
(Hebrews 5:10)

37 x 95 = 3515

3515 = The spirit of Jesus Christ, πνευματος Ιησου
Χριστου, (Phil. 1:19)

37 x 96 = 3552

3552 = The source of eternal salvation, αιτιος σωτηριας
αιωνιου, (Hebrews 5:9)

3552 = The mystery of God, του μυστηριου του Θεου,
(Col. 2:2)

37 x 98 = 3626

3626 = This is my body (Christ's), τουτο εστιν το
σωμαμου, (Matthew 26:26)

37 x 101 = 3737

3737 = Jesus Christ the son of David, *Ιησου Χριστου ο*
       υιου Δαυιδ, (Matthew 1:1)

3737 = The God of our fathers, *ο Θεος των πατερων*
       ημων, (Acts 22:14)

37 x 115 = 4255

4255 = The firstborn from the dead (the resurrected Jesus),
       ο πρωτοτοκος των νεκρων, (Revelation 1:5)

37 x 124 = 4588

4588 = The Prince of the kings of the earth (Jesus),
       ο αρχων των βασιλεων της γης, (Revelation 1:5)

37 x 131 = 4847

4847 = God who quickeneth all things, *του Θεου του*
       ζωογονουν τος τα παντα, (I Timothy 6:13)

37 x 223 = 8251

8251 = In Him was life, and the life was the light of men,
       εν αυτω ζωη ην και η ζωη ην το φως των
       ανθρωπων, (John 1:4)

Bibliography

David Baron, *Types, Psalms, and Prophecies,* Yanetz Ltd., Jerusalem, Israel, 1978

E. W. Bullinger, *Number in Scripture,* Kregel Publications, Grand Rapids, Michigan, U.S.A., 1967

Michael Drosnin, *The Bible Code,* Simon & Schuster, New York, NY, U.S.A., 1997

Bonnie Gaunt, *Stonehenge...a closer look,* Bonnie Gaunt, Jackson, Michigan, U.S.A., 1979

———————— *The Magnificent Numbers of the Great Pyramid and Stonehenge,* Bonnie Gaunt, Jackson, Michigan. U.S.A., 1985

———————— *The Stones Cry Out,* Bonnie Gaunt, Jackson, Michigan, U.S.A., 1991

———————— *Stonehenge and the Great Pyramid: Window on the Universe,* Bonnie Gaunt, Jackson, Michigan, U.S.A., 1993

———————— *Beginnings: the Sacred Design,* Bonnie Gaunt, Jackson, Michigan, U.S.A., 1995

H. E. Huntley, *The Divine Proportion,* Dover Publications, New York, U.S.A., 1970

Robert Lawler, *Sacred Geometry,* Crossroad, New York, NY, U.S.A., 1982

Greg Rigby, *On Earth As It Is In Heaven,* Rhaedus Publications, Guernsey, UK, 1996

Michael S. Schneider, *A Beginner's Guide to Constructing the Universe,* Harper Collins Publishers, New York, NY, U.S.A., 1994

Joseph A. Seiss, *The Gospel in the Stars,* Kregel Publications, Grand Rapids, Michigan, U.S.A., 1972

William Stirling, *The Canon,* Research Into Lost Knowledge Organisation, London, UK, 1981

Del Washburn & Jerry Lucas, *Theomatics*, Stein & Day, New York, U.S.A., 1977

PHILOSOPHY & RELIGION

TIME AND THE BIBLE'S NUMBER CODE
An Exciting Confirmation of God's Time-Line
by Bonnie Gaunt

Bonnie Gaunt's latest research confirms the authenticity of the Bible's Number Code (Gematria) in this latest book of all new material. Gaunt delve into the fascinating patterns of time and numbers that reveal, she says, the master plan of the "Great Mathematician" to create the Kingdom of God on Earth. Confirming the time-line using the Number Code and the beautiful Golden Proportion is the exciting theme of this book. Chapters include Finding a New Method; Why 6,000 Years?; The Year 1999 and 5760; The Pilgrim Festivals; Confirmation of Time Blocks; Jubilees—a Countdown "Seven Times" (The Amazing Golden Proportion); Putting It All Together; more.
200 PAGES. 5x8 PAPERBACK. ILLUSTRATED. APPENDIX. $14.95. CODE: TBNC

THE STONES AND THE SCARLET THREAD
New Evidence from the Bible's Number Code, Stonehenge & the Great Pyramid
by Bonnie Gaunt

Researcher Bonnie Gaunt's latest work confirms the authenticity of the Bible's Number Code (Gematria). New evidence has been found linking its amazing pattern of numbers and its time prophecies with the sacred geometry of ancient stone structures such as Stonehenge and the Great Pyramid. In this, her ninth book, Gaunt builds on the research presented in her previous eight books, and brings to light new evidence that a Master Plan involving man and his future on planet earth has been in the process from the beginning. She shows, through the Number Code, that the Bible's ancient story of the scarlet thread has been intricately woven through the history and future of man. The exciting book will open new vistas of understanding and insight into the marvelous works of the Master Designer.
224 PAGES. 5x8 PAPERBACK. ILLUSTRATED. APPENDIX. $14.95. CODE: SST

THE BIBLE'S AWESOME NUMBER CODE!
by Bonnie Gaunt

Researcher Bonnie Gaunt continues her research on Gematria and Bible codes. In this book, Gaunt details a new discovery of the numeric patterns in the Gematria of the Bible and their relationship to the 3:4:5: triangle, and the earth, moon and sun. Using the Number Code, it is found that the parable of the Good Samaritan is, in fact, a time prophecy, telling the time of Jesus' return. His miracles of healing and of turning water into wine have been encoded with evidence of the time and the work of the beginning of the great "Third Day." The Number Code takes us on a journey from Bethlehem to Golgotha, and into the Kingdom of Jesus Christ, the Kingdom of God and the building of the New Jerusalem. According to Gaunt, these awesome numbers also reveal the great "Third Day" as beginning in the Hebrew Year 5760 (AD 1999-2000).

220 PAGES. 5X8 PAPERBACK. ILLUSTRATED. $14.95. CODE: BANC

The
BIBLE'S
awesome
NUMBER
CODE!

1234567890
Bonnie Gaunt

BEGINNINGS
the Sacred Design

BEGINNINGS
The Sacred Design
by Bonnie Gaunt

Bonnie Gaunt continues the line of research begun by John Michell into the geometric design of Stonehenge, the Great Pyramid and the Golden Proportions. Chapters in this book cover the following topics: the amazing number 144 and the numbers in the design of the New Jerusalem; the Great Pyramid, Stonehenge and Solomon's Temple display a common design that reveals the work of a Master Designer; the amazing location of Bethlehem; how the process of photosynthesis reveals the sacred design while transforming light into organic substance; how the Bible's number code (gematria) reveals a sacred design; more.
211 PAGES. 6X8 PAPERBACK. ILLUSTRATED. $14.95. CODE: BSD

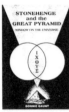

JESUS CHRIST: THE NUMBER OF HIS NAME
The Amazing Number Code Found in the Bible
by Bonnie Gaunt

Gaunt says that the numerological code tells of the new Millennium and of a "Grand Octave of Time" for man. She demonstrates the Bible's number code reveals amazing realities for today's world, and gives evidence of the year of the "second coming" of Jesus Christ. The book reveals amazing evidence that the code number for Jesus Christ has been planted in the geometry of the Earth, ancient megalithic buildings in Egypt, Britain and elsewhere, and in the Bible itself. Gaunt examines the mathematics of the Great Pyramid, Stonehenge, and the city of Bethlehem, which she says bears the number of Jesus in its latitude and longitude. Discover the hidden meaning to such number codes in the Bible as 666, 888, 864, 3168, and more.
197 PAGES. 6x9 PAPERBACK. ILLUSTRATED. BIBLIOGRAPHY. $14.95. CODE: JCNN

STONEHENGE AND THE GREAT PYRAMID
Window on the Universe
by Bonnie Gaunt

Mathematician and theologist Bonnie Gaunt's study on the Sacred Geometry of Stonehenge and the Great Pyramid. Through architecture, mathematics, geometry and the ancient science of "measuring," man can know the secrets of the Universe as encoded in these ancient structures. This is a fascinating study of the geometry and mathematics encompassed in these amazing megaliths as well as the prophecy beliefs surrounding the inner chambers of the Great Pyramid, the gematria of the Bible and how this translates into numbers which are also encoded within these structures. Interest is high in ancient Egypt at the moment, with attention focused on how old the Sphinx and Great Pyramid really are. Additionally, the current crop circle phenomenon is centered around Stonehenge.
216 PAGES. 6X8 PAPERBACK. ILLUSTRATED. $14.95. CODE: SAGP

STONEHENGE ...A CLOSER LOOK
by Bonnie Gaunt

Like the Great Pyramid, Stonehenge is steeped in mystery and is a masterwork in stone. Gaunt decodes the megaliths and tells not only of 4,000 years of history, but of the timeless forces of the universe and of the future of this planet.
236 PAGES. 6X8 PAPERBACK. ILLUSTRATED. $9.95. CODE: SCL

24 hour credit card orders—call: 815-253-6390 fax: 815-253-6300
email: auphq@frontiernet.net   www.adventuresunlimitedpress.com   www.wexclub.com

CONSPIRACY & HISTORY

LIQUID CONSPIRACY
JFK, LSD, the CIA, Area 51 & UFOs
by George Piccard
Underground author George Piccard on the politics of LSD, mind control, and Kennedy's involvement with Area 51 and UFOs. Reveals JFK's LSD experiences with Mary Pinchot-Meyer. The plot thickens with an ever expanding web of CIA involvement, from underground bases with UFOs seen by JFK and Marilyn Monroe (among others) to a vaster conspiracy that affects every government agency from NASA to the Justice Department. This may have been the reason that Marilyn Monroe and actress-columnist Dorothy Kilgallen were both murdered. Focusing on the bizarre side of history, *Liquid Conspiracy* takes the reader on a psychedelic tour de force. This is your government on drugs!
264 PAGES. 6x9 PAPERBACK. ILLUSTRATED. $14.95. CODE: LIQC

INSIDE THE GEMSTONE FILE
Howard Hughes, Onassis & JFK
by Kenn Thomas & David Hatcher Childress
Steamshovel Press editor Thomas takes on the Gemstone File in this run-up and run-down of the most famous underground document ever circulated. Photocopied and distributed for over 20 years, the Gemstone File is the story of Bruce Roberts, the inventor of the synthetic ruby widely used in laser technology today, and his relationship with the Howard Hughes Company and ultimately with Aristotle Onassis, the Mafia, and the CIA. Hughes kidnapped and held a drugged-up prisoner for 10 years; Onassis and his role in the Kennedy Assassination; how the Mafia ran corporate America in the 1960s; the death of Onassis' son in the crash of a small private plane in Greece; Onassis as Ian Fleming's archvillain Ernst Stavro Blofeld; more.
320 PAGES. 6x9 PAPERBACK. ILLUSTRATED. $16.00. CODE: IGF

THE ARCH CONSPIRATOR
Essays and Actions
by Len Bracken
Veteran conspiracy author Len Bracken's witty essays and articles lead us down the dark corridors of conspiracy, politics, murder and mayhem. In 12 chapters Bracken takes us through a maze of interwoven tales from the Russian Conspiracy (and a few "extra notes" on conspiracies) to his interview with Costa Rican novelist Joaquin Gutierrez and his Psychogeographic Map into the Third Millennium. Other chapters in the book are A General Theory of Civil War; A False Report Exposes the Dirty Truth About South African Intelligence Services; The New-Catiline Conspiracy for the Cancellation of Debt; Anti-Labor Day; 1997 with selected Aphorisms Against Work; Solar Economics; and more. Bracken's work has appeared in such pop-conspiracy publications as *Paranoia, Steamshovel Press* and the *Village Voice*. Len Bracken lives in Arlington, Virginia and haunts the back alleys of Washington D.C., keeping an eye on the predators who run our country. With a gun to his head, he cranks out his rants for fringe publications and is the editor of *Extraphile*, described by *New Yorker Magazine* as "fusion conspiracy theory."
256 PAGES. 6x9 PAPERBACK. ILLUSTRATED. BIBLIOGRAPHY. $14.95. CODE: ACON.

MIND CONTROL, WORLD CONTROL
by Jim Keith
Veteran author and investigator Jim Keith uncovers a surprising amount of information on the technology, experimentation and implementation of mind control. Various chapters in this shocking book are on early CIA experiments such as Project Artichoke and Project R.H.I.C.-EDOM, the methodology and technology of implants, mind control assassins and couriers, various famous Mind Control victims such as Sirhan Sirhan and Candy Jones. Also featured in this book are chapters on how mind control technology may be linked to some UFO activity and "UFO abductions."
256 PAGES. 6x9 PAPERBACK. ILLUSTRATED. FOOTNOTES. $14.95. CODE: MCWC

NASA, NAZIS & JFK:
The Torbitt Document & the JFK Assassination
introduction by Kenn Thomas
This book emphasizes the links between "Operation Paper Clip" Nazi scientists working for NASA, the assassination of JFK, and the secret Nevada air base Area 51. The Torbitt Document also talks about the roles played in the assassination by Division Five of the FBI, the Defense Industrial Security Command (DISC), the Las Vegas mob, and the shadow corporate entities Permindex and Centro-Mondiale Commerciale. The Torbitt Document claims that the same players planned the 1962 assassination attempt on Charles de Gaul, who ultimately pulled out of NATO because he traced the "Assassination Cabal" to Permindex in Switzerland and to NATO headquarters in Brussels. The Torbitt Document paints a dark picture of NASA, the military industrial complex, and the connections to Mercury, Nevada which headquarters the "secret space program."
258 PAGES. 5x8. PAPERBACK. ILLUSTRATED. $16.00. CODE: NNJ

MIND CONTROL, OSWALD & JFK:
Were We Controlled?
introduction by Kenn Thomas
Steamshovel Press editor Kenn Thomas examines the little-known book *Were We Controlled?*, first published in 1968. The book's author, the mysterious Lincoln Lawrence, maintained that Lee Harvey Oswald was a special agent who was a mind control subject, having received an implant in 1960 at a Russian hospital. Thomas examines the evidence for implant technology and the role it could have played in the Kennedy Assassination. Thomas also looks at the mind control aspects of the RFK assassination and details the history of implant technology. A growing number of people are interested in CIA experiments and its "Silent Weapons for Quiet Wars." Looks at the case that the reporter Damon Runyon, Jr. was murdered because of this book.
256 PAGES. 6x9 PAPERBACK. ILLUSTRATED. NOTES. $16.00. CODE: MCOJ

ATLANTIS REPRINT SERIES

ATLANTIS: MOTHER OF EMPIRES
Atlantis Reprint Series
by Robert Stacy-Judd
Robert Stacy-Judd's classic 1939 book on Atlantis is back in print in this large-format paperback edition. Stacy-Judd was a California architect and an expert on the Mayas and their relationship to Atlantis. He was an excellent artist and his work is lavishly illustrated. The eighteen comprehensive chapters in the book are: The Mayas and the Lost Atlantis; Conjectures and Opinions; The Atlantean Theory; Cro-Magnon Man; East is West; And West is East; The Mormons and the Mayas; Astrology in Two Hemispheres; The Language of Architecture; The American Indian; Pre-Panamanians and Pre-Incas; Columns and City Planning; Comparisons and Mayan Art; The Iberian Link; The Maya Tongue; Quetzalcoatl; Summing Up the Evidence; The Mayas in Yucatan.
340 PAGES. 8x11 PAPERBACK. ILLUSTRATED. INDEX. $19.95. CODE: AMOE

MYSTERIES OF ANCIENT SOUTH AMERICA
Atlantis Reprint Series
by Harold T. Wilkins
The reprint of Wilkins' classic book on the megaliths and mysteries of South America. This book predates Wilkin's book *Secret Cities of Old South America* published in 1952. *Mysteries of Ancient South America* was first published in 1947 and is considered a classic book of its kind. With diagrams, photos and maps, Wilkins digs into old manuscripts and books to bring us some truly amazing stories of South America: a bizarre subterranean tunnel system; lost cities in the remote border jungles of Brazil; legends of Atlantis in South America; cataclysmic changes that shaped South America; and other strange stories from one of the world's great researchers. Chapters include: Our Earth's Greatest Disaster, Dead Cities of Ancient Brazil, The Jungle Light that Shines by Itself, The Missionary Men in Black: Forerunners of the Great Catastrophe, The Sign of the Sun: The World's Oldest Alphabet, Sign-Posts to the Shadow of Atlantis, The Atlanean "Subterraneans" of the Incas, Tiahuanacu and the Giants, more.
236 PAGES. 6x9 PAPERBACK. ILLUSTRATED. INDEX. $14.95. CODE: MASA

SECRET CITIES OF OLD SOUTH AMERICA
Atlantis Reprint Series
by Harold T. Wilkins
The reprint of Wilkins' classic book, first published in 1952, claiming that South America was Atlantis. Chapters include Mysteries of a Lost World; Atlantis Unveiled; Red Riddles on the Rocks; South America's Amazons Existed!; The Mystery of El Dorado and Gran Payatiti—the Final Refuge of the Incas; Monstrous Beasts of the Unexplored Swamps & Wilds; Weird Denizens of Antediluvian Forests; New Light on Atlantis from the World's Oldest Book; The Mystery of Old Man Noah and the Arks; and more.
438 PAGES. 6x9 PAPERBACK. ILLUSTRATED. BIBLIOGRAPHY & INDEX. $16.95. CODE: SCOS

THE SHADOW OF ATLANTIS
The Echoes of Atlantean Civilization Tracked through Space & Time
by Colonel Alexander Braghine
First published in 1940, *The Shadow of Atlantis* is one of the great classics of Atlantis research. The book amasses a great deal of archaeological, anthropological, historical and scientific evidence in support of a lost continent in the Atlantic Ocean. Braghine covers such diverse topics as Egyptians in Central America, the myth of Quetzalcoatl, the Basque language and its connection with Atlantis, the connections with the ancient pyramids of Mexico, Egypt and Atlantis, the sudden demise of mammoths, legends of giants and much more. Braghine was a linguist and spends part of the book tracing ancient languages to Atlantis and studying little-known inscriptions in Brazil, deluge myths and the connections between ancient languages. Braghine takes us on a fascinating journey through space and time in search of the lost continent.
288 PAGES. 6x9 PAPERBACK. ILLUSTRATED. $16.95. CODE: SOA

THE HISTORY OF ATLANTIS
by Lewis Spence
Lewis Spence's classic book on Atlantis is now back in print! Spence was a Scottish historian (1874-1955) who is best known for his volumes on world mythology and his five Atlantis books. *The History of Atlantis* (1926) is considered his finest. Spence does his scholarly best in chapters on the Sources of Atlantean History, the Geography of Atlantis, the Races of Atlantis, the Kings of Atlantis, the Religion of Atlantis, the Colonies of Atlantis, more. Sixteen chapters in all.
240 PAGES. 6x9 PAPERBACK. ILLUSTRATED WITH MAPS, PHOTOS & DIAGRAMS. $16.95. CODE: HOA

ATLANTIS IN SPAIN
A Study of the Ancient Sun Kingdoms of Spain
by E.M. Whishaw
First published by Rider & Co. of London in 1928, this classic book is a study of the megaliths of Spain, ancient writing, cyclopean walls, sun worshipping empires, hydraulic engineering, and sunken cities. An extremely rare book, it was out of print for 60 years. Learn about the Biblical Tartessus; an Atlantean city at Niebla; the Temple of Hercules and the Sun Temple of Seville; Libyans and the Copper Age; more. Profusely illustrated with photos, maps and drawings.
284 PAGES. 6x9 PAPERBACK. ILLUSTRATED. $15.95. CODE: AIS

THE MYSTERY OF EASTER ISLAND
by Katherine Routledge

The reprint of Katherine Routledge's classic archaeology book which was first published in London in 1919. The book details her journey by yacht from England to South America, around Patagonia to Chile and on to Easter Island. Routledge explored the amazing island and produced one of the first-ever accounts of the life, history and legends of this strange and remote place. Routledge discusses the statues, pyramid-platforms, Rongo Rongo script, the Bird Cult, the war between the Short Ears and the Long Ears, the secret caves, ancient roads on the island, and more. This rare book serves as a sourcebook on the early discoveries and theories on Easter Island.

432 PAGES. 6X9 PAPERBACK. ILLUSTRATED. $16.95. CODE: MEI

MYSTERY CITIES OF THE MAYA
Exploration and Adventure in Lubaantun & Belize
by Thomas Gann

First published in 1925, *Mystery Cities of the Maya* is a classic in Central American archaeology-adventure. Gann was close friends with Mike Mitchell-Hedges, the British adventurer who discovered the famous crystal skull with his adopted daughter Sammy and Lady Richmond Brown, their benefactress. Gann battles pirates along Belize's coast and goes upriver with Mitchell-Hedges to the site of Lubaantun where they excavate a strange lost city where the crystal skull was discovered. Lubaantun is a unique city in the Mayan world as it is built out of precisely carved blocks of stone without the usual plaster-cement facing. Lubaantun contained several large pyramids partially destroyed by earthquakes and a large amount of artifacts. Gann shared Mitchell-Hedges belief in Atlantis and lost civilizations (pre-Mayan) in Central America and the Caribbean. Lots of good photos, maps and diagrams.

252 PAGES. 6X9 PAPERBACK. ILLUSTRATED. $16.95. CODE: MCOM

IN SECRET TIBET
by Theodore Illion

Reprint of a rare 30s adventure travel book. Illion was a German wayfarer who not only spoke fluent Tibetan, but travelled in disguise as a native through forbidden Tibet when it was off-limits to all outsiders. His incredible adventures make this one of the most exciting travel books ever published. Includes illustrations of Tibetan monks levitating stones by acoustics.

210 PAGES. 6X9 PAPERBACK. ILLUSTRATED. $15.95. CODE: IST

DARKNESS OVER TIBET
by Theodore Illion

In this second reprint of Illion's rare books, the German traveller continues his journey through Tibet and is given directions to a strange underground city. As the original publisher's remarks said, "this is a rare account of an underground city in Tibet by the only Westerner ever to enter it and escape alive! "

210 PAGES. 6X9 PAPERBACK. ILLUSTRATED. $15.95. CODE: DOT

IN SECRET MONGOLIA
by Henning Haslund

First published by Kegan Paul of London in 1934, Haslund takes us into the barely known world of Mongolia of 1921, a land of god-kings, bandits, vast mountain wilderness and a Russian army running amok. Starting in Peking, Haslund journeys to Mongolia as part of the Krebs Expedition—a mission to establish a Danish butter farm in a remote corner of northern Mongolia. Along the way, he smuggles guns and nitroglycerin, is thrown into a prison by the new Communist regime, battles the Robber Princess and more. With Haslund we meet the "Mad Baron" Ungern-Sternberg and his renegade Russian army, the many characters of Urga's fledgling foreign community, and the last god-king of Mongolia, Seng Chen Gegen, the fifth reincarnation of the Tiger god and the "ruler of all Torguts." Aside from the esoteric and mystical material, there is plenty of just plain adventure: Haslund encounters a Mongolian werewolf; is ambushed along the trail; escapes from prison and fights terrifying blizzards; more.

374 PAGES. 6X9 PAPERBACK. ILLUSTRATED. BIB. & INDEX. $16.95. CODE: ISM

MEN & GODS IN MONGOLIA
by Henning Haslund

First published in 1935 by Kegan Paul of London, Haslund takes us to the lost city of Karakota in the Gobi desert. We meet the Bodgo Gegen, a god-king in Mongolia similar to the Dalai Lama of Tibet. We meet Dambin Jansang, the dreaded warlord of the "Black Gobi." There is even material in this incredible book on the Hi-mori, an "airhorse" that flies through the sky (similar to a Vimana) and carries with it the sacred stone of Chintamani. Aside from the esoteric and mystical material, there is plenty of just plain adventure: Haslund and companions journey across the Gobi desert by camel caravan; are kidnapped and held for ransom; witness initiation into Shamanic societies; meet reincarnated warlords; and experience the violent birth of "modern" Mongolia.

358 PAGES. 6X9 PAPERBACK. ILLUSTRATED. INDEX. $15.95. CODE: MGM

LOST CITIES

TECHNOLOGY OF THE GODS
The Incredible Sciences of the Ancients
by David Hatcher Childress

Popular *Lost Cities* author David Hatcher Childress takes us into the amazing world of ancient technology, from computers in antiquity to the "flying machines of the gods." Childress looks at the technology that was allegedly used in Atlantis and the theory that the Great Pyramid of Egypt was originally a gigantic power station. He examines tales of ancient flight and the technology that it involved; how the ancients used electricity; megalithic building techniques; the use of crystal lenses and the fire from the gods; evidence of various high tech weapons in the past, including atomic weapons; ancient metallurgy and heavy machinery; the role of modern inventors such as Nikola Tesla in bringing ancient technology back to modern use; impossible artifacts; and more.

356 PAGES. 6x9 PAPERBACK. ILLUSTRATED. BIBLIOGRAPHY. $16.95. CODE: TGOD

VIMANA AIRCRAFT OF ANCIENT INDIA & ATLANTIS
by David Hatcher Childress, introduction by Ivan T. Sanderson

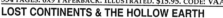

Did the ancients have the technology of flight? In this incredible volume on ancient India, authentic Indian texts such as the *Ramayana* and the *Mahabharata* are used to prove that ancient aircraft were in use more than four thousand years ago. Included in this book is the entire Fourth Century BC manuscript *Vimaanika Shastra* by the ancient author Maharishi Bharadwaaja, translated into English by the Mysore Sanskrit professor G.R. Josyer. Also included are chapters on Atlantean technology, the incredible Rama Empire of India and the devastating wars that destroyed it. Also an entire chapter on mercury vortex propulsion and mercury gyros, the power source described in the ancient Indian texts. Not to be missed by those interested in ancient civilizations or the UFO enigma.

334 PAGES. 6x9 PAPERBACK. ILLUSTRATED. $15.95. CODE: VAA

LOST CONTINENTS & THE HOLLOW EARTH
I Remember Lemuria and the Shaver Mystery
by David Hatcher Childress & Richard Shaver

Lost Continents & the Hollow Earth is Childress' thorough examination of the early hollow earth stories of Richard Shaver and the fascination that fringe fantasy subjects such as lost continents and the hollow earth have had for the American public. Shaver's rare 1948 book *I Remember Lemuria* is reprinted in its entirety, and the book is packed with illustrations from Ray Palmer's *Amazing Stories* magazine of the 1940s. Palmer and Shaver told of tunnels running through the earth—tunnels inhabited by the Deros and Teros, humanoids from an ancient spacefaring race that had inhabited the earth, eventually going underground, hundreds of thousands of years ago. Childress discusses the famous hollow earth books and delves deep into whatever reality may be behind the stories of tunnels in the earth. Operation High Jump to Antarctica in 1947 and Admiral Byrd's bizarre statements, tunnel systems in South America and Tibet, the underground world of Agartha, the belief of UFOs coming from the South Pole, more.

344 PAGES. 6x9 PAPERBACK. ILLUSTRATED. $16.95. CODE: LCHE

LOST CITIES OF NORTH & CENTRAL AMERICA
by David Hatcher Childress

Down the back roads from coast to coast, maverick archaeologist and adventurer David Hatcher Childress goes deep into unknown America. With this incredible book, you will search for lost Mayan cities and books of gold, discover an ancient canal system in Arizona, climb gigantic pyramids in the Midwest, explore megalithic monuments in New England, and join the astonishing quest for lost cities throughout North America. From the war-torn jungles of Guatemala, Nicaragua and Honduras to the deserts, mountains and fields of Mexico, Canada, and the U.S.A., Childress takes the reader in search of sunken ruins, Viking forts, strange tunnel systems, living dinosaurs, early Chinese explorers, and fantastic lost treasure. Packed with both early and current maps, photos and illustrations.

590 PAGES. 6x9 PAPERBACK. ILLUSTRATED. FOOTNOTES & BIBLIOGRAPHY. $16.95. CODE: NCA

LOST CITIES & ANCIENT MYSTERIES OF SOUTH AMERICA
by David Hatcher Childress

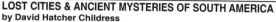

Rogue adventurer and maverick archaeologist David Hatcher Childress takes the reader on unforgettable journeys deep into deadly jungles, high up on windswept mountains and across scorching deserts in search of lost civilizations and ancient mysteries. Travel with David and explore stone cities high in mountain forests and hear fantastic tales of Inca treasure, living dinosaurs, and a mysterious tunnel system. Whether he is hopping freight trains, searching for secret cities, or just dealing with the daily problems of food, money, and romance, the author keeps the reader spellbound. Includes both early and current maps, photos, and illustrations, and plenty of advice for the explorer planning his or her own journey of discovery.

381 PAGES. 6x9 PAPERBACK. ILLUSTRATED. FOOTNOTES. BIBLIOGRAPHY. $14.95. CODE: SAM

LOST CITIES & ANCIENT MYSTERIES OF AFRICA & ARABIA
by David Hatcher Childress

Across ancient deserts, dusty plains and steaming jungles, maverick archaeologist David Childress continues his world-wide quest for lost cities and ancient mysteries. Join him as he discovers forbidden cities in the Empty Quarter of Arabia; "Atlantean" ruins in Egypt and the Kalahari desert; a mysterious, ancient empire in the Sahara; and more. This is the tale of an extraordinary life on the road: across war-torn countries, Childress searches for King Solomon's Mines, living dinosaurs, the Ark of the Covenant and the solutions to some of the fantastic mysteries of the past.

423 PAGES. 6x9 PAPERBACK. ILLUSTRATED. FOOTNOTES & BIBLIOGRAPHY. $14.95. CODE: AFA

24 hour credit card orders—call: 815-253-6390 fax: 815-253-6300

email: auphq@frontiernet.net   www.adventuresunlimitedpress.com   www.wexclub.com

LOST CITIES

LOST CITIES OF ATLANTIS, ANCIENT EUROPE & THE MEDITERRANEAN
by David Hatcher Childress

Atlantis! The legendary lost continent comes under the close scrutiny of maverick archaeologist David Hatcher Childress in this sixth book in the internationally popular *Lost Cities* series. Childress takes the reader in search of sunken cities in the Mediterranean; across the Atlas Mountains in search of Atlantean ruins; to remote islands in search of megalithic ruins; to meet living legends and secret societies. From Ireland to Turkey, Morocco to Eastern Europe, and around the remote islands of the Mediterranean and Atlantic, Childress takes the reader on an astonishing quest for mankind's past. Ancient technology, cataclysms, megalithic construction, lost civilizations and devastating wars of the past are all explored in this book. Childress challenges the skeptics and proves that great civilizations not only existed in the past, but the modern world and its problems are reflections of the ancient world of Atlantis.
524 PAGES. 6x9 PAPERBACK. ILLUSTRATED WITH 100S OF MAPS, PHOTOS AND DIAGRAMS. BIBLIOGRAPHY & INDEX. $16.95. CODE: MED

LOST CITIES OF CHINA, CENTRAL INDIA & ASIA
by David Hatcher Childress

Like a real life "Indiana Jones," maverick archaeologist David Childress takes the reader on an incredible adventure across some of the world's oldest and most remote countries in search of lost cities and ancient mysteries. Discover ancient cities in the Gobi Desert; hear fantastic tales of lost continents, vanished civilizations and secret societies bent on ruling the world; visit forgotten monasteries in forbidding snow-capped mountains with strange tunnels to mysterious subterranean cities! A unique combination of far-out exploration and practical travel advice, it will astound and delight the experienced traveler or the armchair voyager.
429 PAGES. 6x9 PAPERBACK. ILLUSTRATED. FOOTNOTES & BIBLIOGRAPHY. $14.95. CODE: CHI

LOST CITIES OF ANCIENT LEMURIA & THE PACIFIC
by David Hatcher Childress

Was there once a continent in the Pacific? Called Lemuria or Pacifica by geologists, Mu or Pan by the mystics, there is now ample mythological, geological and archaeological evidence to "prove" that an advanced and ancient civilization once lived in the central Pacific. Maverick archaeologist and explorer David Hatcher Childress combs the Indian Ocean, Australia and the Pacific in search of the surprising truth about mankind's past. Contains photos of the underwater city on Pohnpei; explanations on how the statues were levitated around Easter Island in a clockwise vortex movement; tales of disappearing islands; Egyptians in Australia; and more.
379 PAGES. 6x9 PAPERBACK. ILLUSTRATED. FOOTNOTES & BIBLIOGRAPHY. $14.95. CODE: LEM

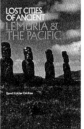

ANCIENT TONGA
& the Lost City of Mu'a
by David Hatcher Childress

Lost Cities series author Childress takes us to the south sea islands of Tonga, Rarotonga, Samoa and Fiji to investigate the megalithic ruins on these beautiful islands. The great empire of the Polynesians, centered on Tonga and the ancient city of Mu'a, is revealed with old photos, drawings and maps. Chapters in this book are on the Lost City of Mu'a and its many megalithic pyramids, the Ha'amonga Trilithon and ancient Polynesian astronomy, Samoa and the search for the lost land of Havai'iki, Fiji and its wars with Tonga, Rarotonga's megalithic road, and Polynesian cosmology. Material on Egyptians in the Pacific, earth changes, the fortified moat around Mu'a, lost roads, more.
218 PAGES. 6x9 PAPERBACK. ILLUSTRATED. COLOR PHOTOS. BIBLIOGRAPHY. $15.95. CODE: TONG

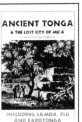

ANCIENT MICRONESIA
& the Lost City of Nan Madol
by David Hatcher Childress

Micronesia, a vast archipelago of islands west of Hawaii and south of Japan, contains some of the most amazing megalithic ruins in the world. Part of our *Lost Cities* series, this volume explores the incredible conformations on various Micronesian islands, especially the fantastic and little-known ruins of Nan Madol on Pohnpei Island. The huge canal city of Nan Madol contains over 250 million tons of basalt columns over an 11 square-mile area of artificial islands. Much of the huge city is submerged, and underwater structures can be found to an estimated 80 feet. Islanders' legends claim that the basalt rocks, weighing up to 50 tons, were magically levitated into place by the powerful forefathers. Other ruins in Micronesia that are profiled include the Latte Stones of the Marianas, the menhirs of Palau, the megalithic canal city on Kosrae Island, megaliths on Guam, and more.
256 PAGES. 6x9 PAPERBACK. ILLUSTRATED. INCLUDES A COLOR PHOTO SECTION. BIBLIOGRAPHY. $16.95. CODE: AMIC

24 hour credit card orders—call: 815-253-6390 fax: 815-253-6300
email: auphq@frontiernet.net   www.adventuresunlimitedpress.com   www.wexclub.com

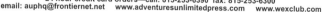

One Adventure Place
P.O. Box 74
Kempton, Illinois 60946
United States of America
Tel.: 815-253-6390 • Fax: 815-253-6300
Email: auphq@frontiernet.net
http://www.adventuresunlimitedpress.com
or www.wexclub.com/aup

ORDERING INSTRUCTIONS

✓ Remit by USD$ Check, Money Order or Credit Card
✓ Visa, Master Card, Discover & AmEx Accepted
✓ Prices May Change Without Notice
✓ 10% Discount for 3 or more Items

SHIPPING CHARGES

United States

✓ Postal Book Rate { $3.00 First Item
                     50¢ Each Additional Item
✓ Priority Mail { $4.00 First Item
                  $2.00 Each Additional Item
✓ UPS { $5.00 First Item
         $1.50 Each Additional Item
   NOTE: UPS Delivery Available to Mainland USA Only

Canada

✓ Postal Book Rate { $6.00 First Item
                     $2.00 Each Additional Item
✓ Postal Air Mail { $8.00 First Item
                    $2.50 Each Additional Item
✓ Personal Checks or Bank Drafts MUST BE
  USD$ and Drawn on a US Bank
✓ Canadian Postal Money Orders OK
✓ Payment MUST BE USD$

All Other Countries

✓ Surface Delivery { $10.00 First Item
                     $4.00 Each Additional Item
✓ Postal Air Mail { $14.00 First Item
                    $5.00 Each Additional Item
✓ Payment MUST BE USD$
✓ Checks and Money Orders MUST BE USD$
  and Drawn on a US Bank or branch.
✓ Add $5.00 for Air Mail Subscription to
  Future Adventures Unlimited Catalogs

SPECIAL NOTES

✓ RETAILERS: Standard Discounts Available
✓ BACKORDERS: We Backorder all Out-of-
  Stock Items Unless Otherwise Requested
✓ PRO FORMA INVOICES: Available on Request
✓ VIDEOS: NTSC Mode Only. Replacement only.
✓ For PAL mode videos contact our other offices:

European Office:
Adventures Unlimited, Panewaal 22,
Enkhuizen, 1600 AA, The Netherlands
http: www.adventuresunlimited.nl
Check Us Out Online at:
www.adventuresunlimitedpress.com

Please check: ☑

☐ This is my first order   ☐ I have ordered before   ☐ This is a new address

Name				
Address				
City				
State/Province		Postal Code		
Country				
Phone day	Evening			
Fax				

Item Code	Item Description	Price	Qty	Total

Please check: ☑

☐ Postal-Surface
☐ Postal-Air Mail
   (Priority in USA)
☐ UPS
   (Mainland USA only)

Subtotal ➡	
Less Discount-10% for 3 or more items ➡	
Balance ➡	
Illinois Residents 6.25% Sales Tax ➡	
Previous Credit ➡	
Shipping ➡	
Total (check/MO in USD$ only) ➡	

☐ Visa/MasterCard/Discover/Amex

Card Number

Expiration Date

10% Discount When You Order 3 or More Items!

Comments & Suggestions	Share Our Catalog with a Friend